GW00384168

SUSSEX

Above Amberley Wildbrooks. The water meadows inspired one of the loveliest piano pieces by the composer John Ireland (1879-1962), who lived nearby and is buried at Shipley.

Following page Chalk, clay and sand: a view north from Harting Down across the gently undulating Weald to the sandstone ridge which, at Black Down, forms the highest point in Sussex.

SUSSEX

THE COUNTY IN COLOUR

TEXT BY DAVID ARSCOTT
PHOTOGRAPHS BY TERRY HEATHCOTE

THE DOVECOTE PRESS

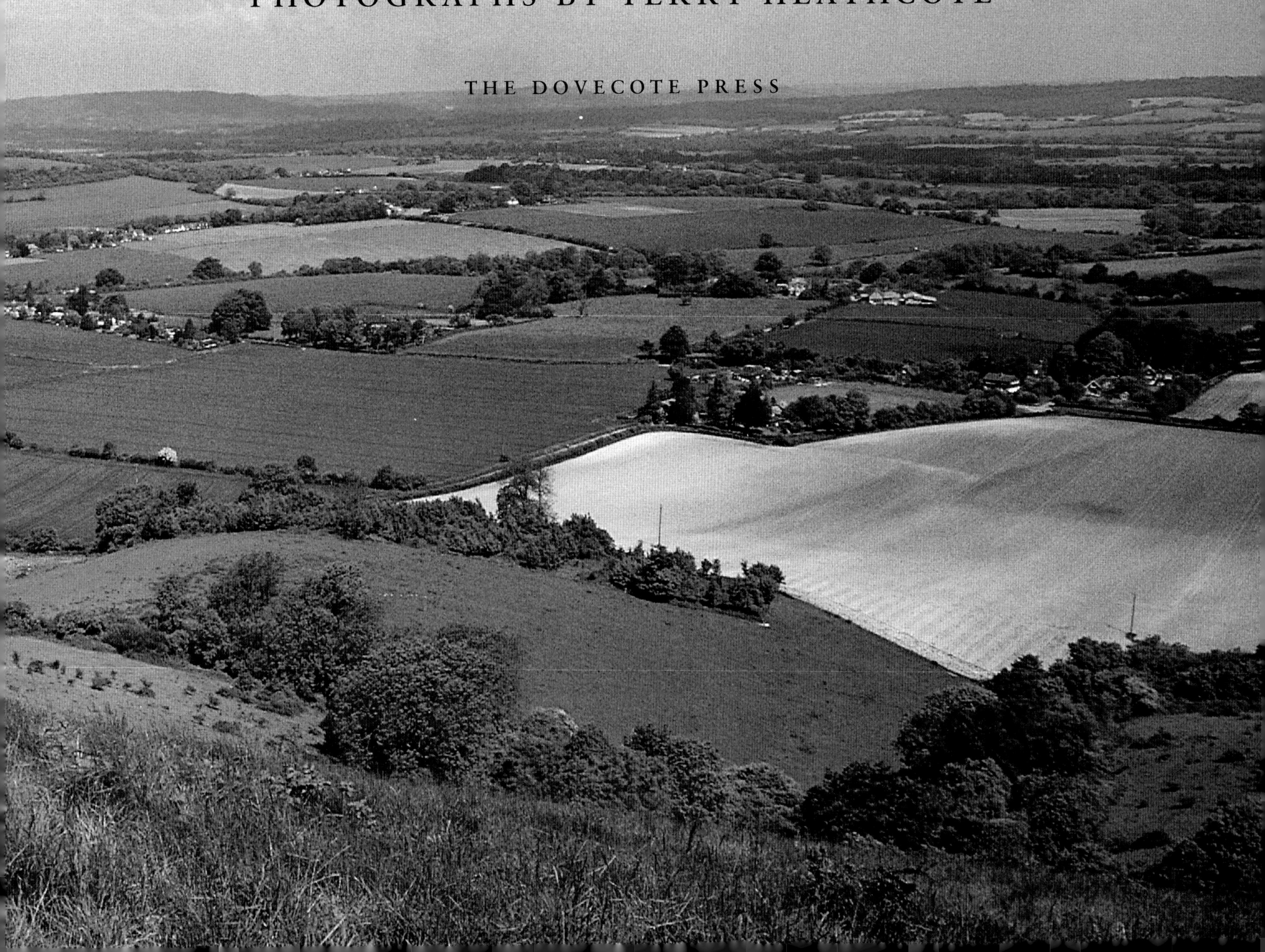

Churchyard and timber-framed houses in Church Square, Rye.

First published in 1995 by The Dovecote Press Ltd
Stanbridge, Wimborne, Dorset BH21 4JD

ISBN 1 874336 32 6

Designed by The Dovecote Press

Photoset in Sabon by The Typesetting Bureau, Wimborne, Dorset
Printed and bound in Singapore

British Library Cataloguing-in-Publication Data
A catalogue record of this book is
available from the British Library

CONTENTS

SUSSEX

RUDYARD KIPLING, that uncrowned laureate of Sussex, famously declared that 'the Weald is good, the Downs are best', but those of us who love the improbable variety of this jumbled countryside will always suspect that so rash a verdict must have been dictated by the arm-twisting necessities of rhyme. His Puck of Pook's Hill, after all, was quite properly unable to decide which he loved the most, 'the Weald or the Marsh or the white Chalk coast'. As for Hilaire Belloc, Kipling's only rival as a singer of Sussex songs, he admirably hedged his bets in 'The South Country', a poem which variously eulogises the county's woods, hills, sea coast and sandy heaths. There is no need to choose.

It was the upward thrust of massive earth movements many millions of years ago that produced the kaleidoscopic scenery we enjoy today. Sedimentary rocks originally laid down in an orderly vertical sequence beneath the waters of freshwater lakes and the sea were violently rearranged, the oldest of them pushed up at the centre of the great 'Wealden anticline', the youngest peeled away to the rim, until all of them were now exposed to the elements, lying side by side in narrow horizontal bands running roughly east to west. Weathering and the works of man did the rest, ensuring that although our two writers lived but 35 miles apart (Kipling in the east, Belloc in the west), their immediate surroundings were very different. Sussex is several miniature landscapes in one.

Belloc's home was at Shipley in the Low Weald, a broad, gently undulating belt of heavy clay, once legendary for its impassability, which runs along the northern perimeter of the Downs east from the River Arun as far as the fringes of Pevensey Levels. The clay grows massive oaks and much of it is ideal for the making of bricks and tiles: the typical vernacular Wealden house is timber-framed and tile-hung, its roof sagging from the weight of large sandstone slabs.

Sandstone of various kinds is plentiful in Sussex, but when Belloc travelled west beyond the Arun he soon came to a landscape quite unknown in Kipling's east: the insect-rich sandy heathlands of the Petworth/Midhurst region, open tracts of heather and bracken with scatterings of birch and pine. This is lower greensand country, the ground rising to 919ft at Black Down near the Surrey border, the highest point in Sussex. Tennyson lived here, at Aldworth House, and wrote a simple, but memorable, quatrain for a friend:

You came and looked and loved the view
Long known and loved by me,
Green Sussex, fading into blue,
With one grey glimpse of sea.

If Belloc travelled south over the chalk Downs to that sea he was on distinctive terrain once again. The flat coastal plain which extends from Shoreham west to the spread-fingered inlets of Chichester Harbour lies, from the geological point of view, quite outside the rest of Sussex. This land of gravels, fertile sands and clays was once sub-

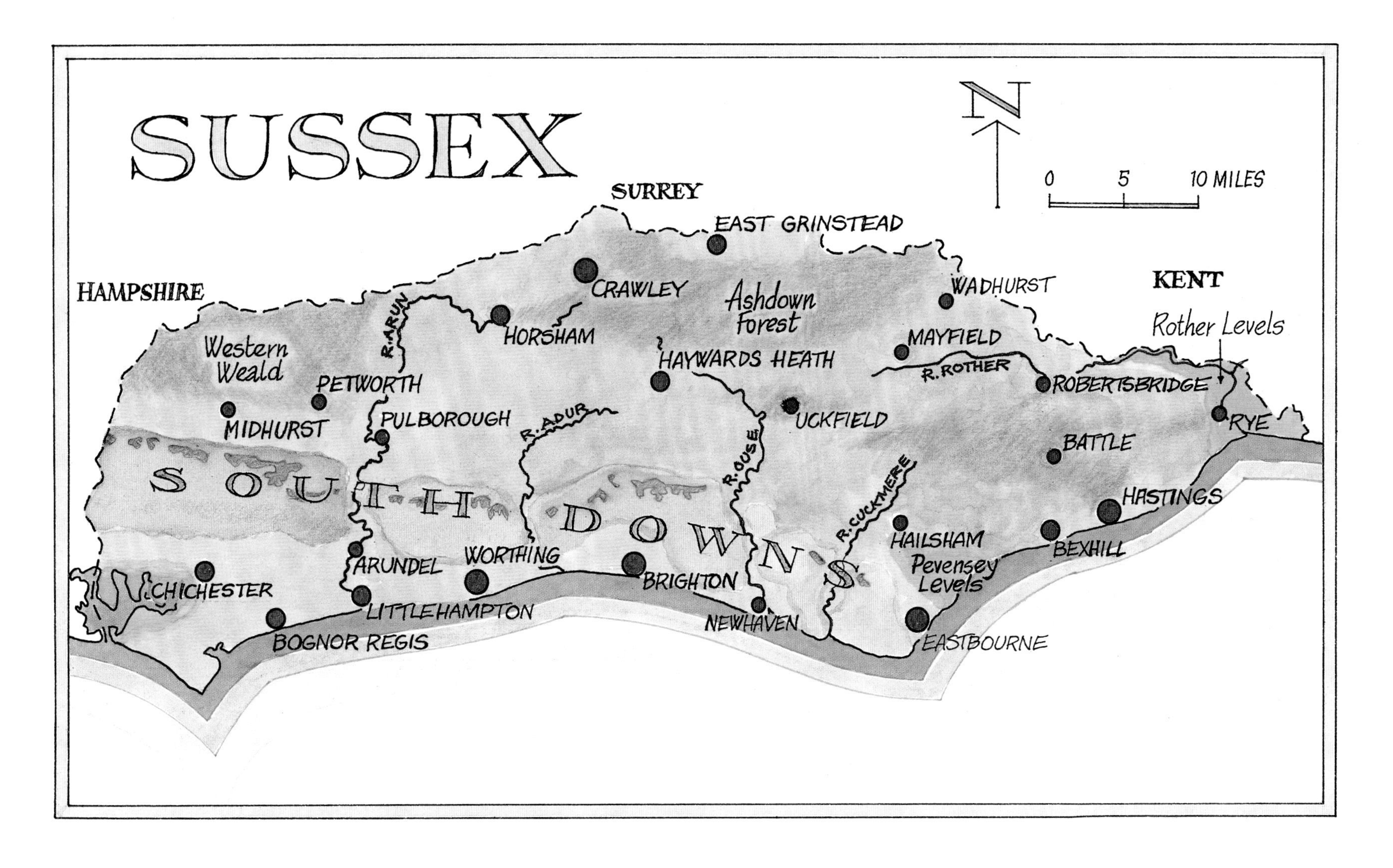

merged below the waves: remnants of an ancient chalk cliff can be traced along the 200ft contour line several miles inland.

Kipling lived at Burwash in the High Weald, Kent border country with scatterings of oast houses and, still today, a few farms where hops are grown. The two principal underlying rocks here are tough sandstone and the more readily weathered Wadhurst clay, a combination which has produced a dramatic landscape of steep hills and deep valleys, with villages perched on the hilltops or, like Burwash itself, strung out along the ridges.

The marshes Kipling knew best were those east of Rye, where the lonely, sheep-grazed flatlands of Sussex (far wetter, and therefore richer in aquatic wildlife, before the introduction of efficient modern drainage) run into those of Kent with not the slightest clue that a border has been crossed. But East Sussex has Pevensey Levels, too, and the west has nothing to compare with either.

What the two writers had in common, of course, was a prospect of Downs to the south, but even here there were differences. In the towns and villages of the chalk country, both would find walls, cottages, even substantial houses, attractively built of the local flint, but Kipling's hills are 'blunt, bow-headed, whale-backed' because they are largely bereft of trees, whereas Belloc dreams of 'walking in the high woods' of his leafy western Downs.

Many of the handsome, spreading beeches were planted by the owners of vast estates which remain more or less intact today: the feudal tradition is much weaker in East Sussex.

If, as seems desirable, our two authors are to meet on neutral territory, Kipling should be invited to head north west from Burwash while Belloc strikes north east from Shipley, each taking one of the many sunken, winding lanes which are characteristic of the Weald. Belloc climbs steadily to St Leonards Forest, then proceeds due east across the wooded Forest Ridge, passing to the south of Crawley (a mere village in his day) and East Grinstead. Kipling having successfully skirted Crowborough, perhaps with a sociable nod towards Sir Arthur Conan Doyle's house, the two men will at last, and to mutual delight, shake hands on the heathy, windblown eminence of Ashdown Forest – preferably, I should say, at the spot where A. A. Milne had Christopher Robin, Winnie the Pooh and their friends enjoying a life of eternal innocence.

These varied landscapes have been inhabited, traversed and written about for so long that Sussex really ought to have no secrets at all. Prehistoric men and women, indelibly scarring the Downs with their causewayed camps, burial mounds, flint mines and hillforts, were followed in their turn by the Roman, Saxon and Norman settlers whose works can likewise still be seen all about us. During the sixteenth and seventeenth centuries the Weald was a clangorous industrial centre, with glass-making in the Kirdford area and an iron industry which demanded vast quantities of timber for fuel, and which dammed rivers to form the large hammerponds that drove the hammers and bellows.

With a coastline so close to the capital, Sussex has also served often enough as London's doormat, its inhabitants long accustomed to shaking off the dust of passing armies, traders and general pleasure-seekers. But the sea has brought prosperity to the county, too: through its ports (Shoreham and Newhaven are our only remaining commercial harbours); illegally through rampant smuggling; most recently with the rise of the seaside resorts which, for good or ill, have spread like a rash all along the Channel coast over the past two hundred years.

And yet this landscape does still retain its secrets. Most of us, after all, take the direct route to our pleasures, and the highest concentration of tourist attractions (as of population) is crowded into the one narrow coastal strip which, whatever its virtues, is far from typical of Sussex as a whole. To travel beyond it, as Terry Heathcote's wonderful photographs surely urge us to do, is to realise that this is the most wooded county in England; that some eighty per cent of it is actively farmed; and that there are secluded places without number which many a Sussex resident, let alone the holiday-maker, has never discovered.

'I found,' recounts Kipling's narrator in the evocative Sussex-based short story *They*, 'hidden villages where bees, the only things awake, boomed in eighty-foot lindens that overhung grey Norman churches; miraculous brooks diving under stone bridges built for heavier traffic than would ever vex them again; tithe-barns larger than their churches, and an old smithy that cried out aloud how it had once been a hall of the Knights of the Temple.'

This hidden Sussex, defying the ravages of time, yet remains to be enjoyed.

DAVID ARSCOTT
Westmeston

CHICHESTER THE HARBOURS AND THE COASTAL PLAIN

CHICHESTER, THE HARBOURS AND THE COASTAL PLAIN

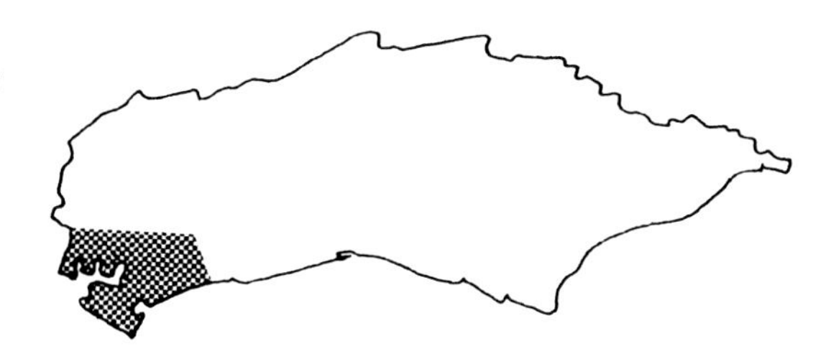

REMOTE as it may be from the rest of the county, the flat and watery land from which the spire of Chichester Cathedral rises like a beacon was the very cradle of Sussex civilisation. It was in this area that the conquering Romans established a military base from which to launch their relentless advance to the west from AD43, with a deep water harbour at Fishbourne where their client-king Cogidubnus built his gorgeous palace. They created the town of Noviomagus, now Chichester, as their trading and administrative centre, and for almost four centuries made of the coastal plain and its fringing downland slopes a vast granary.

It was here, too, that Christianity took root in Saxon Sussex – although the county has the dubious distinction of being the very last in England to accept the faith. St Wilfrid came ashore in the Selsey area in 681 and later built a monastery on a site now covered by the waves. The bishopric he founded at Selsey was transferred to Chichester by the Normans in 1075.

Chichester, although it reveals ample evidence of its Roman origins – the walls can still be walked in places – is essentially a Georgian city. Many of the older houses were

Previous page Edward Story, bishop of Chichester from 1478, gave the people of Chichester their ornate, octagonal market cross in 1501, just two years before he died. It sits at the meeting of four streets which divide the city into quadrants – a legacy of Roman town planning. On the east face is a bronze statue of Charles I, set up after the Restoration. Bishop Story also endowed the Prebendal School in West Street, where the cathedral choristers are educated. His tomb, under a carved and painted canopy, lies close to the altar in the Cathedral.

Left The coastguard lookout rises above wave-borne shingle at Selsey Bill, once known as Seal's Island and the southernmost point of Sussex. Half a mile of land has been drowned here since Domesday, and the monastery founded by St Wilfrid is one of many buildings long lost beneath the sea. Wilfrid established a diocese for the South Saxons at Selsey and it remained here until 1075, when the Normans removed it to Chichester. It was at Selsey, on July 25th, 1588, that the great Spanish Armada was first spotted sailing towards the Sussex coast.

Looking south-west from Halnaker Mill. Wherever you find yourself on the extensive coastal plain, your eyes will constantly be drawn to Chichester's distant cathedral spire.

rebuilt or refaced during a period of great prosperity which began early in the eighteenth century, when a boom in the corn trade brought farmers, merchants and the professional classes flocking to the city. The Pallant area is particularly fine: Nairn and Pevsner, in their celebrated *Buildings of England* volume on Sussex, rightly describe this unspoilt enclave as 'a kind of village-inside-the-city'.

The sea, with its perpetual comings and goings, is the undisputed master of the coastal plain. Once it covered everything below the Downs as far east as Shoreham, and the rich soils it left in its wake have combined with a mild climate to make this a fertile horticultural region. But it still hungrily reclaims land, too, and several roads which now run down to the water's edge originally led to settlements long gone.

Bungaloid sprawl is a common feature of the Sussex coastline, and there is more than enough of it along this stretch, but the two harbours make ample amends. Pagham Harbour, by far the smaller, is a notable nature reserve, attracting vast flocks of wildfowl, particularly in the winter months. Chichester Harbour has a similar range of wildlife habitats, but its 17 miles of navigable creeks and channels also make it an ideal playground for pleasure sailors of every age and degree of experience.

Chichester Cathedral, the only medieval English cathedral visible from the sea, was begun by Bishop Ralph de Luffa in 1091 and is thoroughly Romanesque in feeling. Despite serious damage caused by fires in 1114 and again in 1187 (the consequent weakening of the mortar still causes problems today), work continued throughout the twelfth century, and the building was at last consecrated in 1199. Whereas the original material was chiefly a greenish limestone from Quarr Abbey on the Isle of Wight, masons in the late twelfth and thirteenth centuries used Caen stone from northern France. It was presumably the threat of structural damage which, during the late fourteenth century, led to the construction of one of the cathedral's most unusual features, the country's only surviving example of a detached bell-tower. Some five hundred years later that precautionary move was shown to be fully justified: on February 21st, 1861 (on the very day that a local newspaper poured scorn on 'absurd reports circulating as to the danger of the spire falling'), the central tower spectacularly collapsed. Among the cathedral's ancient treasures are two carved stone panels thought to date from 1130, while modern works include a vivid tapestry reredos by John Piper, a painting by Graham Sutherland and a richly coloured window by Marc Chagall.

Right Few county towns have tamed the car as successfully as Chichester, and the area around the Market Cross is completely pedestrianised. East Street, pictured here, has the Georgian look which typifies the city's architecture, although most of the buildings are, in fact, modern copies of the style.

Left Boats moored along the Chichester Canal. Canals had a brief and less than glorious fling in Sussex during the early nineteenth century. The roads were notoriously appalling in many areas, and the growing need to transport food to London and commodities such as lime and coal to country districts prompted wealthy landowners to improve the navigation of all the major Sussex rivers. The Portsmouth & Arundel Canal, which opened in 1823 with a spur running north into Chichester, joined the Wey and Arun Junction Canal below Arundel, allowing barges to carry goods from the coast right into London. Trade, never very profitable, was killed off within twenty years by the coming of the railway. The eastern end of the canal has disappeared, but the spur and the section west to Chichester Harbour survive, the 8ft-deep lock at Birdham now being used by pleasure craft rather than the sea-going vessels for which it was designed.

Georgian elegance in East Pallant. An economic boom founded on the corn trade in the early eighteenth century completely transformed the medieval squalor of Chichester's south-east quadrant. The Pallant, a crossing of four short streets, was cleared of run-down malthouses and the malodorous warehouses of tanners and fellmongers to become tastefully gentrified. 'The city,' wrote James Spershott, who had witnessed the changes, 'had a very mean appearance in comparison of what it has since arrived to.'

How unfortunate for the dignity of Pallant House, now a public art gallery with collections of paintings, porcelain and sculpture, that two such comical birds should stand guard over it! The house, the finest of its period, was built in the early eighteenth century for the prosperous wine merchant Henry Peckham, whose family crest was graced by ostriches. The unhappy sculptor was handicapped by never having seen such birds in the flesh, and it's hardly surprising that the building has always been known as the Dodo House. Peckham himself must have been mortified to hear the nickname: a young man with pretensions, he banned the market from outside his house and had two fake Elizabethan portraits of his ancestors run up for the drawing room.

The Guildhall Museum in Priory Park, Chichester, was originally the chancel of the thirteenth century Greyfriars church. In 1804 the poet William Blake was tried for sedition here, having allegedly spoken in support of Napoleon Bonaparte while arguing with a soldier at his home in Felpham: he was acquitted. The Greyfriars established their monastery on the site of a delapidated early Norman castle, and a mound in the park marks the site of the keep.

Sir Laurence Olivier was the first director of the Chichester Festival Theatre in Oaklands Park. Founded by a far-sighted local optician, designed by the architects Powell & Moya and completed in 1962, this versatile theatre-in-the-round has from the first attracted outstanding performers and directors, giving it an international reputation. The main house and the smaller studio theatre alongside it offer a year-round programme of music and drama as well as an acclaimed summer season.

The water ought to look more crowded than it does, but the 8,000 pleasure boats moored at Chichester Harbour have 17 miles of navigable creeks and channels to use. There are more than a dozen sailing clubs here, and the only commercial vessels in evidence belong to local fishermen: those on the Hampshire side carry the letter 'P' to indicate their registration in Portsmouth, while those on the Sussex side display 'SM' for Shoreham or 'L' for Littlehampton.

Dell Quay, near the tip of the easternmost arm of the harbour, is a serene backwater today, but this was the port for medieval Chichester – and once ranked as the ninth busiest in the country. Corn was the major export then, with coal, wine and manufactured goods coming in from abroad. Today, inevitably, the old quay and warehouses are the headquarters of a sailing club.

Bosham and its church from the far side of Bosham Channel, one of the main arms of Chichester Harbour. Supposed connections with Canute are, alas, probably fanciful, but it's easy to understand why local legend had it that the king ordered the waves to retreat here. Many of the houses have flood barriers in front of their doors to keep out the lapping water, and motorists who unthinkingly park at the water's edge at low tide sometimes return from a drink or three at the Anchor Bleu to find their cars awash. The steeple-capped tower which stands proud above the waters of Bosham Channel is partly Saxon. It was here that the future King Harold came to pray in 1064 before taking the fateful journey to Normandy which was eventually to prove his undoing at the hands of William the Conqueror: the story is told, and the church is pictured, at the beginning of the Bayeux Tapestry.

Ferries may be a dying mode of transport, but the one that plies between Bosham Hoe and West Itchenor during the season saves a long journey by foot or car. This Cathedral-hull craft, which also serves as a water taxi for yachtsmen, operates at weekends from April to October and daily between mid-July and mid-September.

Charles II kept a yacht at West Itchenor, and many a humble weekend sailor follows in his wake today. Itchenor, with its busy public hard, is the headquarters of the Chichester Harbour Conservancy, which manages the surrounding Area of Outstanding Natural Beauty. It's rather difficult to credit the fact that minesweepers were built here during the Second World War, or that sections of the Mulberry Harbour used for the D-Day landings were fabricated across the water at Bosham.

The largest Roman palace yet discovered west of the Alps was unearthed as recently as 1960, by a workman digging a trench. This was Fishbourne, built for the British tribal leader Cogidubnus who had thrown in his lot with the grateful invading forces in AD 43. The four wings of his palace were arranged around a formal garden whose original bedding trenches have been replanted with the trees and flowers which would have grown here during the years of the Roman peace. The palace itself was destroyed by fire during the late third century, but sufficient remains to suggest the gaudy luxury enjoyed by Cogidubnus and his successors: underfloor heating, elaborately painted walls, marble mouldings and stucco friezes, bronze and marble works of art and (the highlight of a visit today) a series of intricate mosaic floors made of local chalk, limestone and shale.

A Hunter Mk 3 inside the Tangmere Military Aviation Museum, east of Chichester. The RAF Fighter Command aerodrome here played a vital part in the Battle of Britain, and its delapidated control tower still remains as a memory of those courageous times. The airfield's origins can be traced to an emergency landing by Royal Flying Corps pilot Geoffrey Dorman in 1916, and during the 1920s and 30s it was a base for the silver biplane fighters of No 1 and 43 Squadrons. Two hard runways were built just before the Second World War, when Hawker Hurricanes replaced the elegant Gloster Gamecocks, Siskins and Hawker Furies. The Museum, housed in the former radio workshop, contains a rich collection of maps, photographs, uniforms and other relics of the last war. One display features the black-painted Lysander aircraft which carried secret agents in and out of occupied Europe by night. Elsewhere, a large model shows what Tangmere looked like before the afternoon of August 16, 1940, when a large formation of Junkers Ju.87 dive bombers launched a devastating attack on the runways and hangars. Despite this crippling damage, the heroic perseverance of exhausted Hurricane pilots ensured that the airfield remained operational throughout the conflict. Close by, in St Andrews Churchyard, the graves of fallen RAF airmen can be seen alongside those of their former enemies.

Boxgrove Priory. The lovely old church of St Mary the Virgin and St Blaise dates from the early twelfth century when Robert de la Haye, Lord of Halnaker, donated land at Boxgrove to the Benedictine Abbey of Lessay. Inside, the chantry chapel built in 1532 for Lord and Lady de la Warr is the only complete example anywhere in Sussex. With the Dissolution of the Monasteries many of these chantries were defaced, and the de la Warrs bought the church in order to protect theirs. Carvings on the pillars depict themes from the French Book of Hours, including a scene in which a girl holds out her skirt to catch apples scrumped by boys in a tree above her.

The Early English nave of Boxgrove Priory was built around 1220, but the beautiful vaulting dates from the sixteenth century, when Lord de la Warr commissioned Lambert Bernard to paint the arms and crests of his own and his wife's families. A curiosity is the second boss from the east, on which there's a carving of eight faces: there are only eight eyes altogether, yet the design ensures that each face has its full complement of two.

Flooded farmland at Pagham Harbour, a valuable nature reserve which is managed by the county council. The areas of shingle, saltmarsh and mudflat attract large flocks of waders and wildfowl.

Clowns convention, Bognor Regis. What can a small seaside resort do to attract the crowds if, however sandy its beaches, it lacks the reputation and charisma of a Brighton or an Eastbourne? Bognor's solution has been to sponsor the unusual, with an annual gathering of clowns who take their frivolity on to the streets.

The resort was first developed by the London hatter Sir Richard Hotham, who died in 1799 still hoping that the place might be rechristened Hothampton. Several buildings survive from this period, including the Dome in Upper Bognor Road (now occupied by the West Sussex Institute of Higher Education) and a beehive-shaped ice house in London Road which was originally part of the Hotham Estate. It was the patronage of George V, who spent several months recuperating from illness at nearby Craigweil House, which gave the town its 'Regis' suffix in 1929. He certainly liked the place well enough, which ought to make us doubt the story that, consoled on his death bed with the thought of visiting it again, he growled those famous, neatly alliterative, last words: 'Bugger Bognor!'

ARUNDEL AND THE ARUN VALLEY

ARUNDEL AND THE ARUN VALLEY

THE Arun rises in the sandstone country of St Leonard's Forest where its head-waters once fed the hammerponds of wealthy ironmasters. It then runs west to Horsham before turning south across the Weald clay and cutting through the chalk to Arundel, Littlehampton and the sea. Below Pulborough, where the river meets the sprightly little Rother, its flow becomes tidal, and this stretch (together with the fishing rights) has been owned by the Dukes of Norfolk and their predecessors from before Magna Carta. These feudal barons held royal grants to own swans, employing a water bailiff who performed annual swan-upping duties on the Arun: 'Hee is likewise against the second of August yearly being the swann-booking or swan-hopping day to summon owners of swanns that have swan markes on the stream to see their young signetts marked, and taken up if they desire it, paying for marking every signett 4d taking any up 6d.'

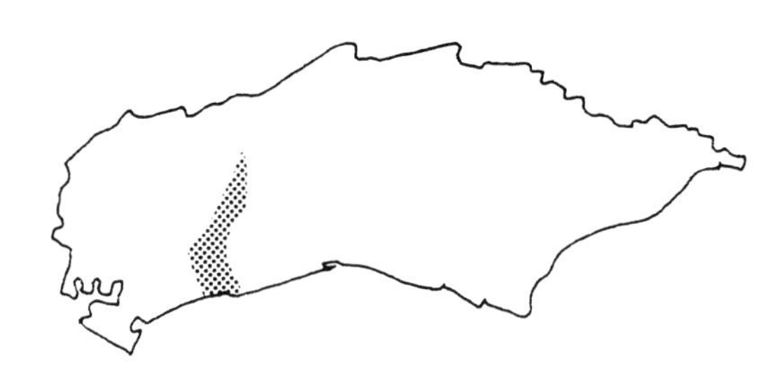

Littlehampton's prosperity once depended upon its harbour, and it had a sizeable ship-building industry towards the end of the eighteenth century, but it was always in competition with its better-connected neighbour a short distance upstream. Henry Fitzalan, an ancestor of the Duke of Norfolk, had cleared and widened the river in the sixteenth century in order to improve Arundel's prospects as a commercial port. In its heyday the town not only handled a wide range of imports but was busy with ship-building yards and a thriving oyster fishery based on shellfish beds in the Channel.

Trade further upriver was encouraged first by cuts and other improvements, later by the creation of the Wey & Arun Junction Canal, completed in 1816 and running north from Pallingham Lock, above Pulborough, into Surrey. Preservationists are now restoring the course of this short-lived enterprise, and a footpath runs alongside for most of its length. The Wey South Path extends south across the lovely water meadows of the Amberley Wildbrooks (impressively rich in plant and bird life) to the picturesque village of Amberley, one of the prettiest in Sussex, with its thatched roofs above flint, timber-framed and whitewashed cottages.

Extensive ramparts on a bend of the river at Burpham are the remains of fortifications built against Viking raids in King Alfred's day. The Normans chose another spot, and parts of their defences survive in the lofty castle at Arundel, which is otherwise largely a restoration begun as recently as 1890. Arundel's imitation French gothic Roman Catholic cathedral, commissioned by the 15th Duke and opened in 1873, was designed by Joseph Aloysius Hansom, better known for his patented safety cab. These buildings give the town a dramatic skyline somewhat at odds with the restfulness of the historic high street, many of whose shops and houses are built on medieval foundations and conceal Tudor timber-framing.

Previous page A view of the Arun east of Arundel Park with the swell of the Downs behind.

Top right Arundel Castle, seen from across the river by the popular Black Rabbit inn. The Wildfowl and Wetlands Trust has established an attractive reserve on the low-lying land below the castle.

Right Arundel's French Gothic skyline is predominantly modern, created by the fifteenth Duke of Norfolk. He had the Roman Catholic parish church of St Philip Neri built to commemorate his coming of age (it was completed in 1873) and in 1965 this became the Cathedral of Our Lady and St Philip Howard, the seat of the Bishop of Arundel and Brighton. The Castle is early Norman in origin – one of the great fortifications built by the conquerors to guard the major river valleys – and the gatehouse is from this period. The twelfth century keep and the medieval, twin-towered barbican still survive, too, but the Castle was badly damaged during the Civil War; first gothicised between 1791 and 1815; and then completely remodelled by the fifteenth Duke from 1890. A highlight of the somewhat chilly interior is the magnificent mahogany library which survives from the eighteenth century restoration.

Above The High Street at Arundel follows the line the Normans chose, climbing a hill in the shadow of the Castle. Today the town is quiet and beautifully maintained, but in the middle of the nineteenth century the Castle was in a state of disrepair and the riverside was noisy with trade. The docks and warehouses have gone, but ships were once built here, and during the Napoleonic wars Arundel was exporting some 60,000 tons of grain a year. Indeed, as recently as the 1930s tall sailing ships came up river from Littlehampton with cargoes of salt, timber and coal, a trade killed by the construction of the railway bridge downriver at Ford in 1935.

Above right The austere grandeur of the Castle and Cathedral at Arundel is countered by the unpretentious simplicity of several narrow streets which occupy the lower ground towards the river. King Street, seen here, runs up to the Cathedral from near the bottom of Maltravers Street, architecturally the most interesting in the town.

Right A carpet of flowers is laid in the nave of Arundel Cathedral each June for the Festival of Corpus Christi.

Ford is best known today for its open prison, on the site of a former airfield, but its little candle-lit flint church, dedicated to St Andrew, is one of the prettiest in the county. The oldest part is the north wall of the nave, which has two small windows dating from the eleventh century, and its outstanding feature is the Norman chancel arch – plain with a star decoration around the supporting masonry. You reach it across a field whose humps and bumps are the remains of a moated manor house.

The simple little church of St Botolph at Hardham holds an amazing treasure for anyone who 'collects' medieval wall paintings – practically a full set of traditional subjects in two tiers. Executed around 1100, these are not only the best to survive anywhere in England, but among the earliest: a scene which shows St George on horseback bearing a lance may represent the Battle of Antioch in 1098, during the first Crusade. The paintings had been plastered over by the thirteenth century and were rediscovered only in 1866, so it is hardly surprising that they lack their original bright colours, but those on the chancel arch are particularly fine. The church itself dates from the eleventh century, but the Romans chose Hardham as the site for the first of their posting stations on the road from Chichester to London and some of their tiles are incorporated in the fabric of the building.

Left Littlehampton may have a large amusements centre on the front, but the greatest natural asset of this most unpretentious of resorts is the vast expanse of golden sand if offers holidaymakers at low tide. The harbour area is the focal point of seafront activity, with a ferry taking passengers across the fast-flowing Arun to the unspoiled West Beach. Inland, along and around the partly-pedestrianised High Street, are several attractive Georgian buildings, including a Friends Meeting House of flint cobbles. This was originally a 'penny school', founded in 1835 by Sarah Mary Welch, who had the misfortune to have been widowed twice within eighteen months. Most pupils paid a penny a week, but Mrs Welch probably subsidised the poorer ones.

Left Stopham Bridge was built over the Arun in 1423 to replace a ferry, and it remained the sole crossing at this point until a new bridge took the heavy traffic away at the end of the 1980s. The finest medieval bridge in Sussex, it has a central arch which was raised in 1822 to allow masted vessels access to the Wey and Arun Junction Canal further upriver. That 23-mile link between the Sussex Arun and the Surrey Wey, which opened in 1816, was constructed in part to facilitate the easy transport of goods which would otherwise have been carried on unsatisfactory roads, but it had another purpose, too: it answered fears that a French fleet under Napoleon might cut off the usual seaward route into London by creating an inland route to the capital from the south coast. This threat never materialised and the canal, which climbed to a height of 163ft above sea level, passing through 26 locks, under 30 bridges and over three aqueducts, was destined to have a short life. The railway gave the *coup de grace* to what had been a briefly successful venture: an Act of Abandonment was passed in 1868 and the canal closed three years later. The Wey and Arun Canal Trust is now expertly restoring considerable lengths of the former waterway.

Above Amberley, mercifully bypassed at the northern end of the Arun gap, is one of the loveliest of Sussex villages, and untypical in its liberal use of thatch. The beautifully maintained cottages display a wide range of materials, including flint, brick, tile, stone and chalk clunch. The four principal lanes form a square, one of them extending to the church and the walls of the castle (now a hotel and restaurant) built for the Bishop of Chichester around 1100 and given its substantial curtain walls in the 1370s when its owners were threatened by both French raiders and rebellious locals. The village has a wonderful location, with the Downs on one side and Amberley Wild Brooks on the other.

Right Jill Belton harvests a colourful crop of Worcester Pearmain apples at Tullens Toat, north of Pulborough. Neighbouring Kent may have awarded itself the title 'The Garden of England', but the north-west of Sussex is a renowned fruit-growing area, too, and the county's first apple-growing cooperative, famous for its Cox's Orange Pippins, was established at Kirdford. The owner of Tullens Toat, David Atkins, has told the colourful story of his conversion from accountant to fruit grower in a book, *The Cuckoo in June*, which has been serialised on Radio 4.

Arthur Haffenden displays the art of besom broom-making at Amberley Chalkpits Museum, a compelling celebration of southern industrial history in the 36 acres of a former working chalk pit next to Amberley Station. The working demonstrations here include printing, pottery and blacksmithing; exhibits cover buses, railways, radio sets, concrete and, of course, chalk pits; and the safety warning in the museum's introductory pamphlet must surely encourage, rather than deter, the average visitor: 'The museum contains equipment and machines that are oily and sometimes give off smuts. Some paths cross railway lines on which trains operate at various times. In some areas machinery is operated, work is carried out on new exhibits, and vehicles move along the roads.' For those not industrially minded there's a nature trail and a number of picnic sites.

The Mens, west of the Arun between Billingshurst and Petworth. A woodland common for a thousand years, this 380-acre nature reserve is among the most primitive areas of woodland in the south of England, supporting some forty species of trees and shrubs, 400 kinds of fungi, 300 flowering herbs and a hundred lichens.

THE HOLIDAY COAST WORTHING TO EASTBOURNE

THE HOLIDAY COAST
WORTHING TO EASTBOURNE

TAKE a decaying fishing port a few miles from a prosperous county town and within convenient reach of the capital; add a craze for healthy sea bathing; and throw in a fun-loving, charismatic Prince Regent. That, in pardonable historical shorthand, was the recipe for the transformation of eighteenth century Brighton and, in a hectic game of follow-my-leader, of almost every settlement of consequence along the Sussex coast. Dr Richard Russell can be said to have started it all in 1750, moving his medical practice the few miles from thriving Lewes to Brighthelmstone (as it was then generally known) and persuasively advocating the sea-water cure. The future George IV first visited the town in 1783 when he was Prince of Wales, and the 'quality' flocked in his wake to enjoy the seasonal round of the baths, theatre, race-course and assembly rooms. The population grew from around two thousand in 1750 to seven thousand in 1800 and close on twenty thousand by 1820.

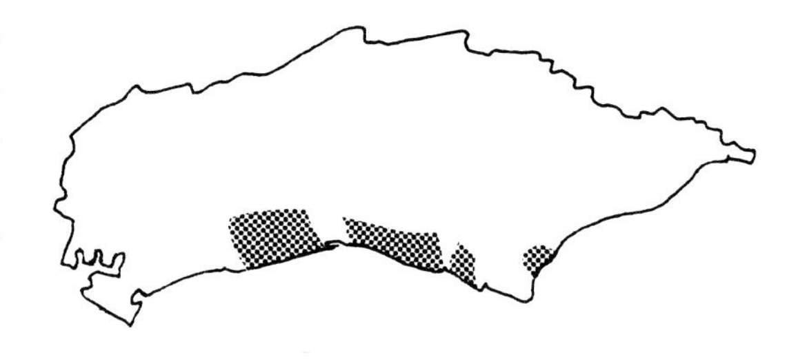

Architects, like the rest of us, tend to let their hair down at the seaside. If the imposing Regency terraces of Brighton and Hove are the most characteristic legacy of this period,

Previous page Poplar Place, Brighton. The brick-paved 'twittens', or narrow alleyways, of The Lanes, with their antique and jewellery shops, are among the town's greatest tourist attractions. The area was first developed during the late sixteenth and early seventeenth century in response to the growth of the fishing industry, and parts of the original houses remain, hidden beneath later rebuilding.

Beach House Park, Worthing. The gentility of this West Sussex resort is neatly symbolised by its leading place in the world of bowls, hosting the national championships on these flawless greens each summer. Worthing's history as a seaside attraction can be precisely dated. On July 31st, 1798, Princess Amelia, the youngest daughter of George III, came here on holiday – escaping from an ill-advised affair with one of her father's equerries. This gave official sanction to the town's reputation as a fashionable watering place, and houses soon began to be built closer to the front to accommodate an influx of well-to-do visitors. Worthing continued to grow, but never embraced the raffishness which is a trademark of Brighton to the east.

West Pier, Brighton. The town for a short period had no fewer than three piers, the earliest being a simple chain pier (a glorified landing stage) which was demolished in a storm in 1896. Today it has only one-and-a-half. While the Palace Pier, begun in 1891, is among the leading tourist venues in the country, the beautiful West Pier is a decaying ruin, its shoreward end removed for reasons of safety. Designed by Eugenius Birch and completed in 1866, it had a deck 1,115ft long for elegant promenading. Various organisations owned it from the 1960s onwards, but none of them found the cash required to replace rusting girders and give it the refurbishment it deserved. In 1975 it was closed, and in 1988 a 110ft section was cut away, isolating the pavilion and concert hall from the shore. The West Pier is, justifiably, the only Grade I listed pier in Britain, and hopes of a highly expensive restoration have remained alive over many years.

the fantastic Indian-style Royal Pavilion designed for 'Prinny' by John Nash is undoubtedly the most bizarre. The Victorians were to add their own colourful embellishments to 'London by the sea', among them two piers, a clock tower above which a time-ball once (noisily) rose and fell on the hour, the Grand and Metropole hotels and the world's first electric railway, still in service today. The seafront awaits its comparable modern extravagances, unless one counts the impressive Yacht Marina at Black Rock, begun in 1971 and one of the largest in Europe.

No other Sussex resort can compete with Brighton for metropolitan raciness, but perhaps none of them would wish to. Worthing began in a similar fashion, a rash of property speculations following the visit of George III's youngest daughter, Princess Amelia, in 1798, but it soon settled for a more genteel existence and is fittingly the national centre for the sedate sport of bowls. Eastbourne, formerly a mere scattering of hamlets, was developed largely by the Earl of Burlington after 1858, when he became the seventh Duke of Devonshire and, overnight, one of the wealthiest men in England. This was a watering place 'built *by* gentlemen *for* gentlemen', with broad, tree-lined boulevards, grassy squares and spacious villas, a vision whose grandeur has survived the piecemeal developments of a shabbier age.

West of Eastbourne as far as the Cuckmere River lies a celebrated area of protected downland, but thereafter the coast is thoroughly developed, the major towns fused with sprawling modern settlements which are rarely better than mediocre from an architectural point of view but which, for many thousands of people, satisfy a dream of living by the sea. The most notorious of these much-derided 'blots on the landscape' is Peacehaven, still displaying traces of its ramshackle frontier-town beginnings – yet, for all that, fiercely defended by its many contented inhabitants.

THE BRIGHTON TOUR
Ice Cream
TOPPERS BAZAAR
HOT FOOD
FISH & CHIPS

Brighton, otherwise known as 'London by the Sea', from the Palace Pier. Arguably the most written-about coastal town in Britain, Brighton has capitalised on its relative proximity to London ever since the sea-water cure and the antics of the Prince Regent established it as a fashionable resort in the late eighteenth century. Before that rebirth it had been a decaying fishing town, still largely confined within its ancient bounds of East Street, North Street, West Street and the sea. Such was the lure of the entertainments on offer (public baths, theatre, race course, assembly rooms) that the population rose from about 7,000 in 1800 to more than 20,000 twenty years later. This popularity extended beyond the Georgian period, which left behind a legacy of imposing seafront terraces, into the Victorian age, which created the Aquarium (now a Sea Life Centre), the Grand and Metropole hotels and the Theatre Royal. Between the wars Brighton earned a reputation for naughtiness (dirty weekends, often contrived for the benefit of would-be divorcees needing evidence for the courts) which still lingers today. Graham Greene, at the beginning of *Brighton Rock,* brilliantly evokes the mood of Bank Holiday visitors: 'They came in by train from Victoria every five minutes, rocked down Queen's Road standing on the tops of the little local trams, stepped off in bewildered multitudes into fresh and glittering air.' The shingle foreshore itself has never been a major part of the attraction, yet in 1980 a stretch of it to the east of the Palace Pier was officially sanctioned as a naturist beach: it isn't heavily populated.

The Grand Hotel on Brighton seafront was built in the 1860s and a hundred years later came close to being demolished to make way for an amusement centre. That indignity survived, it was badly damaged on October 12, 1984, when the IRA exploded a bomb intended to assassinate Prime Minister Margaret Thatcher and her cabinet during the Conservative Party conference: five people were killed and thirty four injured. Within two years a completely restored hotel was reopened by Mrs (now Baroness) Thatcher herself, and new facilities installed in the reconstruction enabled the Grand to become the town's first five-star hotel in 1988.

Many a London-to-Brighton event stages its grand finale along Madeira Drive, east of the Palace Pier, and the veteran car run every November is the most famous of them all. It had its beginnings in the London-to-Brighton Emancipation Run of November 14, 1896, celebrating the repeal of the Locomotives on Highways Act which stipulated that cars should be preceded by a man carrying a red flag: Leon Bollee, driving a Bollee tricycle, was first home in 3hr 44min 35sec. Similar celebration runs were held intermittently in subsequent years until, in 1930, the Veteran Car Club was formed at the Old Ship Hotel on the seafront. Only cars of 1905 or earlier are eligible. Other events which terminate at Madeira Drive each year include the London-to-Brighton cycle ride and the commercial vehicles run, and time trials have been held here, too. The popular promenade and 'carriage drive' was built from 1872 when the new Aquarium was built over the previous sea road.

The Royal Pavilion, Brighton. The Prince Regent's extravagant palace was described by William Hazlitt as a collection of stone pumpkins and pepper boxes, while Dean Swift imagined that St Paul's Cathedral must have pupped on the south coast, but the gaudy fancies of the Pavilion are so outrageous as to be above criticism. The Indian style of the exterior gives way to a predominantly Chinese influence within, the highlight being the music room with its lacquer red and gold, its gigantic serpents and dragons and its great dome of gilded scallop-shaped scales: Rossini entertained the company in this room over Christmas 1823, soon after the building had been completed. Queen Victoria later sold the Pavilion to Brighton Corporation because she preferred the seclusion of Osborne on the Isle of Wight, and after the place had been brutally stripped of all its furnishings and fittings *Punch* magazine suggested that a tea merchant should buy the shell and deck it out with 'a few paper lanterns and a real native at the door'. Today, thanks to a restoration scheme costing millions, the Royal Pavilion can again be seen very much as it was, with some of the original furniture on loan from Buckingham Palace.

Volks Railway, Brighton. The inventor Magnus Volk, son of a German immigrant clockmaker, established the first telephone link in Brighton, fitted the Royal Pavilion with electric lights – and, most famously, built the first electric railway in Britain. It opened on August 4, 1883, less than eight weeks after Volk's first approach to the borough council, and was powered by a 50 volt generator which the inventor had previously used for lighting his home. The first carriage had mahogany sides and blue velvet curtains, conveying a dozen passengers at a speed of 6 mph along a two feet gauge track. A completely new track on a gauge of 2ft 8inches was laid in 1884, maximum speed was increased to 10 mph and the railway was later extended in length – despite opposition from bus operators, taxi drivers and boatmen who were concerned about safety and access to the beach. Carriages dating from 1892 are still in service today on the run of just under two miles from the Palace Pier to the Marina.

Brunswick Square, Hove. The terraces of Regent's Park in London inspired the impressive Regency estates at either end of the Brighton and Hove seafront during the 1820s and 1830s. Brunswick Square and Terrace, to the west in Hove, are matched by Sussex Square and Lewes Crescent in Brighton's Kemp Town, and there are many less substantial developments in between. Grand as they seem, many of these houses were sold as mere shells, their new owners deciding on the disposition of the rooms quite as much as how they should be furnished and decorated.

British Engineerium, Hove. If this remarkable museum may be said to sing a hymn to the ingenuity of the nation's engineers, then the huge beam engines which are 'in steam' every weekend merely whisper the words. One of these practically silent machines pumped water to supply Victorian Brighton and Hove when this building was the Goldstone Pumping Station. Another, which won first prize at the 1889 Parish Exhibition, was saved from decay and brought here from France. Apart from its many exhibits, the Engineerium is an internationally-recognised engineering centre, with a consultancy service for skilled restoration.

Martello Tower, Seaford. An arduous assault on a squat, round tower at Mortella Point, Corsica, in 1794, during the Napoleonic wars, gave the British Army the idea of constructing a chain of 74 similarly sturdy defences along the south coast against possible French invasion – and nobody seemed to have noticed, or cared, that they got the name wrong. Seaford's is the most westerly of them. The towers, although never put to the test by French invaders, have proved difficult to destroy, which no doubt explains why several still remain. Seaford's now serves as an unusual local history museum, with an emphasis on ships and shipwrecks.

Carpet Gardens, Eastbourne. The resort was envisaged as 'a town built *by* gentlemen *for* gentlemen' when it was developed, almost from nothing, after 1858. In that year the Earl of Burlington, who owned some two-thirds of the area, became the seventh Duke of Devonshire and found himself, overnight, one of the wealthiest men in England. With Carew Davies Gilbert, an agricultural innovator and one-time President of the Royal Society who owned about a quarter of the surrounding countryside, he set about creating a town of broad, leafy avenues and roomy villas which, even today, retains a great deal of its original spaciousness. Covenants ensure that the seafront is not commercialised, and the gardens west of the pier are among the greatest attractions for visitors.

Eastbourne from the pier, with the monumental terrace of Grand Parade to the right of the picture. This was built from 1851 and incorporates the Burlington and Claremont Hotels. The Downs begin at the western end of the seafront, a footpath climbing to Beachy Head and the South Downs Way.

Eastbourne's Pier was built in 1872, but a storm five years later swept away the landward end – and this accounts for the difference in levels about a third of the way out. Designed by Eugenius Birch, who was also responsible for the West Pier at Brighton, it stretches a thousand feet out to sea. The Victorian-style entrance was built as recently as 1991.

Eastbourne Town Hall. William Tadman Foulkes of Birmingham won the commission to design this prestigious building in the 1880s, defeating twenty two other architects in the process. He described its restless piling of decorative motifs one upon another as an adaptation of the Renaissance style. The interior is certainly more sumptuous than would be thought fitting today: marble pilasters, oak panelling, stained glass, decorative plaster ceilings and floors of marble mosaic. The most important rooms are on the first floor, among them the mayor's parlour, the town clerk's suite of offices and the council chamber. A band played the Hallelujah Chorus when the building was officially opened on a site which had once housed the parish stocks.

SHOREHAM AND THE ADUR VALLEY

SHOREHAM AND THE ADUR VALLEY

WHILE its neighbours to east and west have grown fat on the money that tourism brings, Shoreham remains faithful to its long history as a working town. The short High Street, with its Georgian customs house, yacht chandlers' shops and slipways to the beach, makes few concessions to the leisure business, and the modern port which stretches all of three miles to the edge of Hove is the largest commercial harbour between Southampton and Dover.

When the Normans arrived here the town was a little way up the River Adur, and they immediately rebuilt the church dedicated to St Nicholas, the patron saint of mariners, giving it transepts, an enlarged chancel and an impressive new tower. This was wasted effort, however, for the settlement was very soon to become known as Old Shoreham: within forty years of the Conquest silting of the river forced the new rulers to start again where Shoreham squats today. The church of St Mary de Haura ('of the harbour') dates

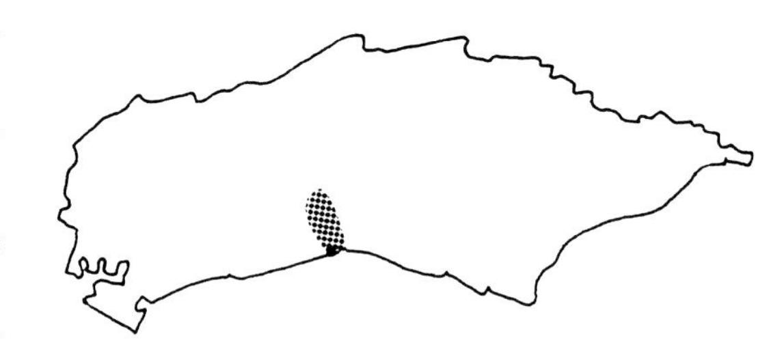

Previous page The eastern arm of the Adur near Wineham. The river rises on Ditchling Common and turns north and west to pass between Haywards Heath and Burgess Hill. Near Henfield it meets the western Adur, which rises in the parish of Slinfold and runs through Shipley and West Grinstead. Below Henfield the Adur flows through the Henfield Levels, an area of unspoilt marshland rich in wildlife, before cutting through the Downs to meet the sea at Shoreham. In earlier times the river was known variously as the Sore, the Beeding, Alder River and Bramber Water. Its present name, first recorded in 1612, is thought to have been invented by an artful scholar in order to identify Shoreham as the south coast harbour (exact location unknown) which Roman writers referred to as Portus Adurni.

The largest commercial harbour between Southampton and Dover, Shoreham nevertheless finds room for pleasure boats. Shingle spits formed over the centuries have created an inland lagoon some three miles long. The town first developed a little way up the Adur, around the church of St Nicholas in Old Shoreham. The Normans rebuilt this Saxon church soon after the Conquest, but by 1100 they had abandoned the site because of the silting up of the estuary, and they built their new town (and the church of St Mary) by the sea, where it is today.

The Marlipins, Shoreham. The attractive stone and flint chequerboard front dates from the fourteenth century, but the building itself is that unusual survivor: an early Norman building which had no religious or military function. Its exact date is unknown, but it may well have been the original Custom House when the de Braose family, who ruled the area from Bramber Castle, ordered the development of New Shoreham at the water's edge. The Marlipins, owned by the Sussex Archaeological Society, is now a maritime history museum.

Shoreham Lighthouse. Drifting shingle spits changed the seaward course of the Adur over the centuries, and the present mouth of the river was fixed, off Kingston Buci, as recently as 1818. The lighthouse was built in 1846, 'serving not only the purpose of pointing out the position of the harbour, but also as a valuable leading light for vessels entering at night.' On mariners' charts of the nineteenth century Kingston is marked as 'Egypt' and Southwick, immediately east, as 'Alexandria'.

from this period, as does the building known as the Marlipins – now faced with fourteenth century chequerboard stone and flint, but one of the original port buildings, perhaps serving as a court or customs house.

The Adur has a great many tributaries, but the two principal streams meet a little to the west of Henfield, a large village with a lively main street and a criss-crossing of leafy footpaths towards the former railway line which is now part of the long-distance Downs Link footpath. The river then runs south through marshland to Bramber, which was a Norman port and administrative centre – a fact which explains the apparently bizarre siting of the once-mighty castle in what is now an insignificant, if attractive, inland village. In medieval times, before persistent silting stifled it, the Adur was still sufficiently wide to justify a magnificent four-arched stone bridge some 170ft long which spanned the water close to the timber-framed house, St Mary's.

After cutting through the Downs in a valley designated an Area of Outstanding Natural Beauty, the river turns east at Shoreham to meet the sea at what used to be called Kingston Buci (after the Norman family of Busci), but which in modern times has been ignorantly, and unimaginatively, rechristened Kingston by Sea. As the shape of the harbour suggests, this was not always its course. Deposits of sand and shingle diverted the rivermouth further and further east from Shoreham over the centuries, until the current exit was artificially established as a permanent feature in 1821 – an initiative which brought a great revival in trade, with large quantities of sea-coal being shipped in from the Durham area and, during the 1850s, oysters being sent by train from Shoreham at the rate of 20,000 tons a year. The picturesque stone lighthouse was built here in 1846.

An Art Deco terminal building from the 1930s graces little Shoreham Airport, which lays claim to being the oldest licensed commercial airfield in the world. The first flight was made in 1910, the flying ground being officially opened as Brighton Aerodrome on June 20, 1911. The land was requisitioned by the Royal Flying Corps during the First World War, after which it was returned to grazing. Scheduled passenger flights began again during the 1930s, only to be interrupted by another world war, when the field became a fighter base. Today the airport has a short hard runway suitable for small passenger aircraft, and is used chiefly for business flights.

Left The magnificent chapel of Lancing College stands high above the River Adur. The college was founded in 1848 by Nathaniel Woodard, curate of Shoreham, but the chapel itself (open daily to the public) took shape only slowly: the rose window at the west end, the largest made during the twentieth century, was installed as recently as the 1980s. At 94ft, the chapel's internal height is exceeded only by Westminster Abbey, York Minster and Liverpool Cathedral. Woodard, whose other schools included Ardingly and Hurstpierpoint Colleges, enlisted powerful financial support for his vision of offering the rising middle classes a Christian education in somewhat spartan conditions at affordable prices. The Woodard schools popularised football in Sussex, and thereby led to the formation of Brighton and Hove Albion in the early 1900s, but a disaffection with the game's professionalism later prompted them to revert to rugby.

Above The lovely little flint-walled church at Coombes is reached through a farmyard and, let deep into the hillside, seems to grow naturally from the ground. The unrestored interior has wall paintings of the same date as those at Hardham and almost certainly executed by the same artists: above the chancel arch is an Atlas-type figure, his face showing the strain of holding up the world. The earliest parts of the church (nave, south doorway and chancel) date from the 11th century.

Bramber Castle, built soon after the Norman Conquest by William de Braose, once defended a busy port several miles inland on the River Adur, then known as Bramber Water. Silting up began as early as the fourteenth century, and the village's former greatness was remembered only in the fact that, until the Reform act of 1832, this 'rotten borough' returned two MPs to Parliament. The Castle, built on a massive natural mound with a moat far down below, quickly fell into disrepair and was used as a quarry for local road building. Today, maintained by English Heritage, it's a popular place for (free) family outings.

The wicked cats holding birds in their paws which decorate the Cat House in Henfield were supposedly intended as a permanent reproach to Canon Nathaniel Woodard, the founder of Lancing College, who lived nearby. Woodard's cat had devoured a canary belonging to the local joiner, Bob Ward, whose house this was. Ward installed a contraption of cats with bells which he jangled loudly every time Woodard hove into view. The house lies off Church Street at Pinchnose Green, so named because there was once a tannery on the site.

Catch 'em young! Children are encouraged to dip for pond life at Woods Mill, the headquarters of the Sussex Wildlife Trust at Small Dole, near Henfield. This 15-acre reserve, billed as 'an ordinary piece of countryside', is home to no fewer than 60 species of breeding birds, 25 species of mammals and more than 260 different plants. The old watermill houses some colourful wildlife displays.

Two views of Steyning. Rather more than a village, not quite a town, Steyning is packed with ancient buildings, many hiding their medieval origins beneath later facades. Its church was founded by St Cuthman in the eighth century, supposedly after the collapse here of the cart in which he was ferrying his ailing mother across the country.

THE SUSSEX DOWNS

THE SUSSEX DOWNS

The Weald is good, the Downs are best –
I'll give you the run of 'em, East to West.
Beachy Head and Winddoor Hill,
They were once and they are still.
Firle, Mount Caburn and Mount Harry
Go back as far as sums'll carry.
Ditchling Beacon and Chanctonbury Ring,
They have looked on many a thing,
And what those two have missed between 'em,
I reckon Truleigh Hill has seen 'em.
Highden, Bignor and Duncton Down
Knew Old England before the Crown.
Linch Down, Treyford and Sunwood
Knew Old England before the Flood...

KIPLING'S rough-hewn verse, celebrating a prehistoric world of causewayed camps, flint mines, burial mounds and Iron Age hillforts, has a stirring final couplet: 'The Downs are sheep, the Weald is corn, You be glad you are Sussex born!' The sad fact of modern economic life is that the Downs are no longer covered with sheep, although conservationists have reintroduced them in some areas in order to preserve the precious wildlife habitat produced by their continuous cropping of otherwise all-smothering tall grasses and infant shrubs. Here the short, springy turf is studded with colourful violets, harebells, cowslips and orchids, fragrant with sweet-smelling herbs such as basil, marjoram and thyme.

The South Downs Way follows an ancient route along the ridge, with the sea to one side and the patchwork fields and woods of the Weald to the other. From a vantage point such as Ditchling Beacon (Kipling by no means included every summit) your view will stretch for many miles on a clear day, the forest ridges backed by a distant view of the North Downs which follow a roughly parallel course through Surrey and Kent. This is good walking country at any season of the year. The turf on its bed of porous chalk quickly dries after rain, and although the Downs have their intersecting valleys (and northern, scarp slopes which are far steeper than those facing the sea), their soft, rounded contours create a gentle and unthreatening environment. West of the Arun, one of four rivers which cut through the Downs on their way to the sea, the predominantly arable landscape gives way to large plantations, with many fine beech trees on pockets of overlying clay. Down below, and always within easy reach, there are ancient settlements with sturdy flint cottages, venerable Norman churches, numerous historic houses and welcoming pubs for the dry of throat and weary of limb.

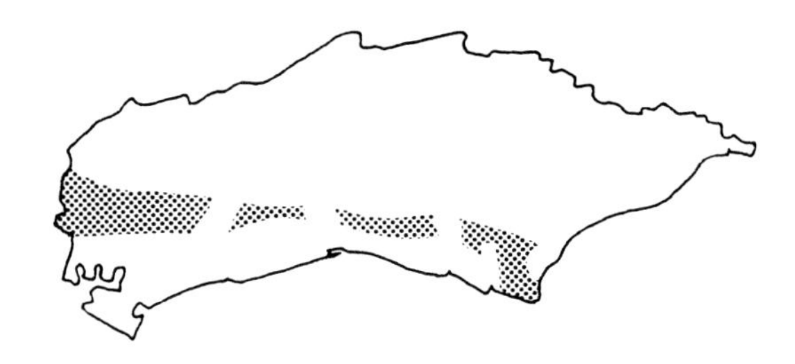

Previous page Devil's Dyke, north of Brighton. The 300ft deep valley, created by a cycle of freeze and thaw after the last Ice Age, is so striking that it inevitably spawned a supernatural legend: the Devil began to dig a vast trench through the Downs one night so that the churches of the Weald would be drowned by the sea, but he mistook an old lady's candle for the rising sun and fled before he could complete the job. Three railways once operated at the Dyke and have left faint traces here: the Dyke Railway, which climbed from Brighton to a station at Devil's Dyke Farm from 1887 until 1934; a steep-grade railway, which ran down the northern slope of the hill to a point west of Poynings village from 1897 until 1908; and a cable railway which carried visitors across the Dyke itself from 1894 until 1909.

Beachy Head, with its lighthouse. The name is derived from the French *beau chef*, or beautiful headland, although the many shipwrecks which litter the seabed in this area explain why Venetian sailors once called it 'The Devil's Cape'. At 534ft, this is the highest point on the south coast, with an unhappy record of suicide attempts – most of them successful.

The church of St Mary at Glynde was built in the Palladian style for Richard Trevor, Bishop of Durham, who lived next door at Glynde Place. The original box pews, west gallery and pulpit of 1763 can still be seen inside. In the graveyard is the tomb of John Ellman (1753-1832), who perfected the Southdown breed of sheep which, in its heyday, was exported to Australia and New Zealand as breeding stock.

Mozart at Glyndebourne. In 1934 the former Eton science master John Christie transformed his family's Tudor country house into an opera house as a stage for his wife, the operatic soprano Audrey Mildmay. The wonder of his achievement was that this loving creation, far from being a self-indulgent folly, rapidly won a worldwide reputation for the quality of its productions. Sixty years to the day after its opening, a new Glyndebourne created by his son, Sir George, gave a repeat performance of the very first work to be produced here: Mozart's *The Marriage of Figaro*. The rebuilt, and lavishly praised, opera house seats 1150 evening dress-attired customers, who still enjoy that famous Glyndebourne tradition, picnicking on the lawn.

The lower photograph is of the 1994 production of *The Marriage of Figaro*, conducted by Bernard Haitink, with Andreas Schmidt (the Count), Gerald Finley (Figaro), Renée Fleming (the Countess) and Alison Hagley (Susanna).

Jack and Jill windmills on the Downs above Clayton. Jack is the black one, a privately-owned tower mill which was built in 1866 and is now part of a house. Jill, a post mill, has been fully restored and is often open to the public at weekends. In common with several other Sussex mills, Jill is not on her original site. First erected in Dyke Road, Brighton, in 1821, some thirty years later she was laboriously trundled to her present position on a trolley sledge dragged by teams of oxen.

Firle Place has been the home of the Gage family since the sixteenth century, but most of what we see today dates from a major restructuring in the eighteenth century. The village itself (properly West Firle, although there is no other) is an endearing cluster of houses and cottages in the lee of the great estate, their twisting lane petering out in a farmyard hard under the Downs. The ill-fated Lt.Gen. Thomas Gage of Firle was commander-in- chief of the British forces at the outbreak of the American War of Independence, and there are several documents of the period on show in the house.

The steeper, north-facing flank of the Downs as seen from Devil's Dyke in hazy high summer, with the Weald stretching out below. The wooded summit of Chanctonbury Ring can be seen in the distance: the trees planted by Charles Goring (son of the local landowner) in 1760 were badly mauled by the 1987 'hurricane', but sufficient survive to make this a landmark for many miles around.

Fulking is one of several downland villages which developed along the spring line, and the clear water gushes out just below the Shepherd and Dog pub. The Biblical quotation on the wellhouse is given a pleasantly rustic touch by the tilesetter's frequent inversion of the letter 'S'. Further up the street is a small drinking fountain which carries a red marble tablet in honour of the Victorian writer and artist John Ruskin (1819-1900), who used his influence to provide villagers with a rather more advanced water supply.

The 'Rhenish helm' cap on the tower of Sompting Church is unique in England, and parts of the building can be dated to half a century before the Norman Conquest. In 1154 the church was granted to the Knights Templars, who virtually rebuilt it. The south transept was their private chapel: 'square and solid as a Crusaders' castle,' the guide book says, 'perhaps built by men who had fought hand to hand with the Saracens in the Holy Land.'

Above A view along the ramparts of Cissbury Ring, one of many Iron Age hillforts whose massive defences are carved into the high points of the South Downs. Man was here much earlier, however, sinking shafts 50ft into the ground to create multi-galleried flint mines: more than two hundred shafts have been identified at Cissbury, where they now appear as a series of dimplings in the turf. At nearby Church Hill, Findon, archaeologists found traces of a wooden ladder used by these neolithic miners, while at Harrow Hill, Angmering, their excavations discovered soot from the miners' lamps on the gallery roofs.

Right A view south from Cissbury Hill.

Left Autumn colour in Slindon Woods. Although the devastating storm of October, 1987, badly damaged the famous beech wood on the National Trust's Slindon estate, many tall specimens remain. Within the wood is a raised shingle beach, showing that the sea level here was once a full 130ft higher than today.

Below Mosaic of Winter at Bignor Roman Villa. The palace at Fishbourne may have been grander, but Bignor has the finer mosaics, including an elaborate head of Medusa in the bath suite. The remains have been open to the public since 1815, four years after a local farmer, George Tupper, unearthed the mosaic of a dancing girl while ploughing.

Opposite top An English idyll: village cricket at Eartham, on the Downs between Arundel and Chichester.

Opposite bottom The tiny twelfth-century apsidal church at Upwaltham is still lit by candles. It was here that the great Cardinal Manning (1808-92) began his religious career as a young curate – and here too that, years later, he preached his last sermon as an Anglican before joining the Roman Catholic church.

Left A medieval shop and a Tudor market hall are among the great survivors grouped around the Market Square at the Weald and Downland Open Air Museum, Singleton. All of the buildings scattered about this partially-wooded 40-acre site were once threatened with destruction or unsympathetic modernisation. Dismantled and patiently reconstructed here, they include farmhouses, a medieval cottage, a village school, a watermill and a number of tradesmen's yards.

Right *Sally is gone that was so kindly,*
Sally is gone from Ha'nacker Hill.
And the Briar grows ever since then so blindly
And ever since then the clapper is still,
And the sweeps have fallen from Ha'nacker Mill.
Belloc's lament still has its resonance, despite the smart new sweeps, for Halnaker Mill is nothing but an empty shell. Built by the Duke of Richmond around 1750 to grind corn for the tenants of his Goodwood estate, this lovable tower mill was restored in 1958 by the County Council. The mill can be reached only on foot, one route being along a remnant of the embankment which flanked the Roman Stane Street, but climbers are rewarded with extensive views to the Selsey peninsula and the Isle of Wight.

Left Festival of Speed at Goodwood. The motor racing circuit on the Goodwood Estate, owned by the Earl of March, once staged Grand Prix events (the crash and serious injuries which Stirling Moss suffered there ended his career), and this event in the grounds of the eighteenth century house celebrates those colourful, if dangerous, days. Better known today is the horse racing course high on the Downs, the highlight of the season being the Glorious Goodwood week every July – 'a garden party with racing tacked on'.

Right The simple flint church of St Mary, North Marden, is nothing but a single room with an apsidal east end, the only one of its kind in Sussex and one of but four in the whole of England. There is an original round-headed Norman window high in the west gable, while the south doorway is twelfth century.

Far right The thirteenth century church of St Michael at Up Marden is completely unspoiled, with what Nairn and Pevsner describe as 'one of the loveliest interiors in England': clear glass windows, pale plaster walls, brick floors and plastered wagon roofs. There are four Mardens (North, East, West and Up), tucked away in beautiful, remote downland countryside. Never large settlements, they dwindled during the latter half of the thirteenth century when cereal growing gave way to less labour-intensive sheep farming on the Downs.

Uppark is not what it seems. A raging fire which swept through the fine seventeenth century house on the afternoon of August 30, 1989, had reduced it to a smoking shell by first light the following day. Firemen wearing breathing apparatus brought out scarcely recognisable treasures which a chain of volunteers passed to the safety of the lawn. What we now see, outside and in, is very largely a reconstruction carried out by the National Trust with meticulous attention to detail, prodigious conservation techniques and the expenditure of some twenty million pounds.

Uppark's remarkable collection of furniture, pictures and porcelain, much of which can now be enjoyed again, was acquired by Sir Matthew Fetherstonhaugh, who bought the house in 1747 after inheriting a vast fortune and subsequently went on the Grand Tour through Europe. A later owner had a network of tunnels excavated, linking the servants' working quarters with a detached kitchen building, and allowing food to be carried into the dining room still hot. H.G. Wells lived here as a boy when his mother was housekeeper, and the tunnels are said to have inspired the idea of the time capsule for his novel *The Time Machine*.

THE OUSE VALLEY
LEWES AND NEWHAVEN

THE OUSE VALLEY
LEWES AND NEWHAVEN

DANIEL Defoe described eighteenth century Lewes as 'a fine pleasant town, well built and situated,' adding that it was 'full of gentlemen of good families'. The county town he admired is still recognisable today. The High Street, which clings to the spine of a steep downland spur, is lined with old buildings in a variety of styles and materials and interrupted by numerous ancient, flint-walled alleys ('twittens' to Sussex folk) which plunge down the hillside to the south. Prehistoric and Roman settlers have left their marks on the surrounding countryside, but Lewes was first developed by the Saxons, who established two mints here. The Normans followed suit, building both the castle which, albeit somewhat depleted, proudly waves its flag over the surrounding countryside today, and the massive Cluniac priory whose sorry ruins lie close to the railway line at Southover. Occupying the lowest permanent crossing point of the Ouse, Lewes was an important trading centre throughout the middle ages and beyond, and enjoyed an era of particular prosperity in Georgian times, when corn and livestock poured into its markets from far afield. The town was already a considerable administrative and legal centre, but new banks now sprang up in the High Street, and there were concerts, plays and visits to the races for fashionable visitors who flocked here for the 'season'. Some of the town's finest houses date from this period, many of them faced with so-called mathematical tiles – imitating bricks so realistically that they sometimes fool even the architecturally knowledgeable.

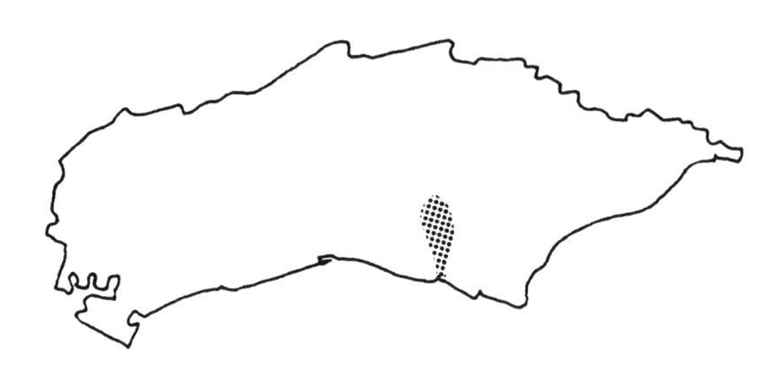

Newhaven, eight miles downstream from Lewes, first became a significant port after 1539 when an artificial cut diverted the straggling Ouse from the silted-up harbour at Seaford to meet the sea at a 'new haven' near the village of Meeching. The town itself has none of the charm of Dieppe, a ferry sailing away across the Channel, but the harbour is colourful enough, with fishing boats moored up against the West Quay.

The river has been put to work in various ways. Where it rises, at Slaugham, it fed an ironmaster's hammerpond, and its course takes it past the sites of several former water-mills – most picturesquely at Barcombe Mills, its tidal limit, where a road built by the Romans still fords the river and where the water ripples and races through a bewildering series of channels and sluices. During the 1790s, several artificial cuts and as many as eighteen locks gave barges access as far inland as Lindfield. The railway soon killed the Upper Ouse Navigation, and this is a quiet waterway today, passing through lovely wealden countryside (and skirting substantial villages such as Balcombe, Ardingly and Lindfield) before cutting through the Downs at Lewes.

Previous page February floodwater at Barcombe Mills. Here the Ouse, one of its tributaries (the Iron River), a canal cut, a mill stream, a series of weirs and two locks now turned into fish ladders create a captivating world of water. A Roman road forded the river from the first or second century, and the bridge across the main course of the Ouse follows its exact line today. There have been mills at Barcombe since Saxon times, and the remains of the last one (a button mill built in 1870 and destroyed by fire in 1939) lie close to the bridge. This spot marks the upper tidal limit of the Ouse, second largest of the Sussex rivers, which rises at Slaugham and meets the sea at Newhaven.

A typical downland cottage of flint with brick quoins at Rodmell.

Lewes and its Castle. The town, which climbs a spur of the Downs with the River Ouse at its foot, has been an important centre since Saxon times.

Lewes Castle, built by the Normans soon after the Conquest, is typical of the period in having a formidable keep on a mound, or motte, with a surrounding yard, or bailey, for the living quarters. The difference here is that Lewes had two mottes, the northern one (Brack Mount) probably having no keep, but protected by a curtain wall: the large grassy hump now stands apart from the considerable remains. The Castle was taken by Simon de Montfort in 1264 when, in the Battle of Lewes, he defeated Henry III and forced the King to accept a treaty which gave the new chartered boroughs representation in Parliament.

Left Southover Grange gardens, Lewes. The Grange, built in 1572, incorporates Caen stone quarried from the ruins of the nearby Cluniac priory. The diarist John Evelyn (1620-1706) spent much of his boyhood here.

Below Anne of Cleves House, Southover. Henry VIII's fourth wife never lived here but, as the owner of Southover manor, she drew an annual rent of seven shillings and sixpence from the property. Now a local history museum run by the Sussex Archaeological Society, the house is essentially sixteenth century, although its tunnel-vaulted cellar is probably two hundred years older.

Lower left Keere Street, with its central paving of 'petrified kidneys', or water-rolled flints. Lewes is riddled with steep twittens, narrow passages between buildings which run at right angles to the High Street and other principal roads. Keere Street, the most celebrated of them, was originally a pathway which fringed a ditch under the town walls. Down this hair-raising slope, legend says, the Prince Regent once drove a coach-and-four for a wager.

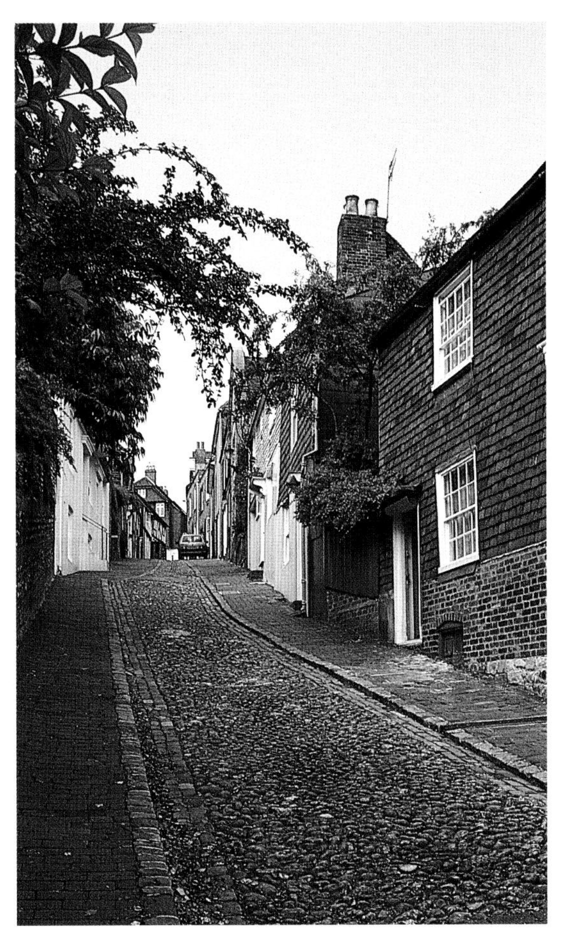

Lewes Bonfire is one of the great events of the English calendar, a wild night of fireworks and blazing tar barrels during which effigies of both Guy Fawkes and the Pope are burned and loudly blown up, together with tableaux featuring contemporary heroes and villains, while mock clerics in robes and mitres stir up the mob. The town supports no fewer than five separate bonfire societies, each of which organises a spectacular fireworks display on November 5 following a seemingly endless Grand Procession from one end of the High Street to the other – a parade which is joined by other bonfire societies from all over Sussex with their attendant bands and banners. Seventeen Protestants were burned at Lewes during the days of Bloody Queen Mary, but the tradition of (now generally good-natured) anti-Catholic sentiment is in fact a product of the nineteenth century, when the Papacy was still regarded as a threat.

Above & right Monks House, Rodmell, for more than twenty years the home of the writer Virginia Woolf (1882-1941) and her husband Leonard (1880-1969). In the garden is a memorial bust which he had erected to her memory after she drowned herself in the Ouse, nearby:

Death is the enemy. "Against you
I will fling myself unvanquished
and unyielding – O Death!"
The waves broke on the shore.

Above A view of St Peter's, Rodmell, from the garden of Monks House. The twelfth century church originally belonged to Lewes Priory, and the fragment of a,shaft with vertical zigzag and a base with spurs is thought to have come from the monks' lavatorium. Rodmell is a small village, in which flint houses and cottages congregate about a single street.

Fishing boats at Newhaven harbour. The fishing fleet has moorings along the West Quay, where the day's catch can be bought.

Newhaven, the only port between Portsmouth and Dover deep enough for large vessels at all states of the tide, has a long-established ferry link with Dieppe. Competition from the Channel Tunnel has reduced the crossing time to less than two hours.

THE CUCKMERE VALLEY

THE CUCKMERE VALLEY

STAND atop the hill called High and Over alongside the Alfriston to Seaford road and the most unspoiled of the major Sussex river valleys stretches beneath your gaze, from the wooded ridges of the Heathfield area some twenty miles northwards, down through the green, pastoral countryside of the Low Weald to the famous meanders which wind sinuously towards the brilliant whiteness of the Seven Sisters cliffs. The Cuckmere's snake-like progress to the sea was bypassed by a cut in 1846 to combat persistent shingle drift, and the river was embanked to lessen flooding in the valley, but there are none of the usual manmade intrusions at this rivermouth: no harbour, no railway, no housing development. To the west a path climbs steeply past former coastguard cottages to the nature reserve on Seaford Head; to the east, the South Downs Way sets off across undulating downland on its way to the gleaming eminence of Beachy Head.

The Seven Sisters Country Park visitors centre at Exceat is an ideal starting point for exploring the area on foot or (since bicycles can be hired here) on two wheels. A level walk of about a mile downstream takes you to the beach, where you can explore rock pools and perhaps find one of the fossil sea urchins which country folk once knew as 'shepherds' crowns', keeping them in their homes for good luck. Immediately to the

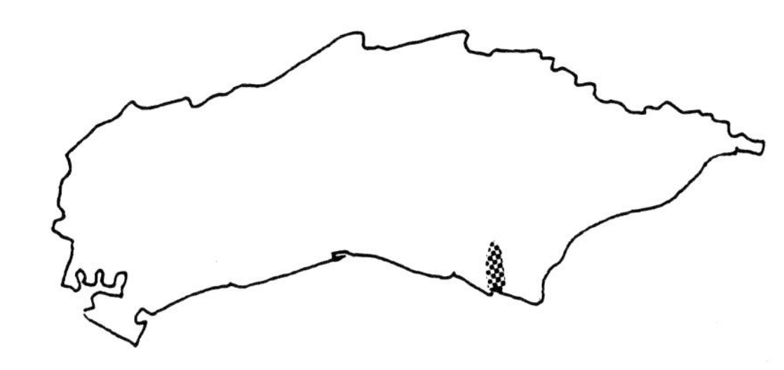

Previous page From Frog Firle, looking east across the River Cuckmere to Litlington. Lullington Heath, on the Downs above the village, is the finest example in Sussex of a 'chalk heath' habitat in which a mixture of soils allows chalk-loving plants to live side by side with those which enjoy acid conditions.

Cuckmere Haven lies between the brilliant white cliffs of Seaford Head, to the west, and the famous Seven Sisters.

The celebrated meanders of the Cuckmere River. The fishing village of Exceat once stood on the higher ground close by, but repeated attacks by French raiders badly damaged it during the medieval period and by the early sixteenth century it had gone: a tablet has been erected by the Sussex Archaeological Society on the site of the old church.

north and east is Friston Forest, an easily accessible beech plantation which has enveloped the beautiful flint-walled village of West Dean, while the journey upriver takes you through a string of pretty hamlets and villages. Alfriston is the most celebrated of these, its narrow main street undeniably far too crowded during the summer months, but its ancient timber-framed houses, market square, inns and tea rooms making it quite irresistible to tourists. The medieval Clergy House, which sits alongside a large green known as The Tye, was the first building ever acquired by the newly-founded National Trust in 1896.

Curiosities of the Cuckmere Valley include what is sometimes tagged 'the smallest church in Sussex' at Lullington (though it is, in fact, the chancel of a decayed medieval building whose remains can still be seen in the turf); the mysterious hill figure carved in the Downs above Wilmington and best viewed from the priory car park; and the modern wall paintings created in the church at Berwick by the 'Bloomsbury' artists Vanessa Bell and Duncan Grant who lived close by at Charleston Farmhouse. At Arlington the river has been diverted from its former wandering course to form a 120-acre reservoir, while at Upper Dicker it feeds the 6-acre moat which surrounds the thirteenth century Michelham Priory.

So famous is the Long Man of Wilmington that the white horse carved into the chalk above Litlington is largely ignored. Almost 90ft long, it was cut as recently as the 1920s and first restored in 1945 after being camouflaged from enemy aircraft during the war.

The large, cruciform church of St Andrew at Alfriston, rather fancifully known as 'the cathedral of the Downs', sits on raised ground within a bend of the river. It was built entirely during the fourteenth century, its walls attractively faced with knapped and squared flints. In past centuries Alfriston practised a moving funeral custom which has been recorded in some other southern counties but not anywhere else in Sussex: after the death of a young girl or of a woman who had had only one husband, a chaplet of white flowers would be carried in front of the coffin, and this 'virgin's wreath' would be hung in the church throughout the following year.

The High Street at Alfriston as few but the local inhabitants have ever seen it! During the season the village is overrun with tourists attracted by its timber-framed shops, inns and tea rooms. The remains of the old market cross can be seen at the far end of the street.

The Clergy House at Alfriston, built for a prosperous yeoman family around 1350, was at one time owned by Michelham Priory; became a vicarage after the Reformation; was later converted into a pair of farm labourers' cottages; and had so fallen into disrepair by 1889 that it was scheduled for demolition. In that year the conservation-minded Rev. F.W. Benyon became the vicar, and he fought to save it despite resounding local apathy: 'Not a shilling has been given inside the parish to preserve the building, whilst Noah when building his ark could scarcely have been subjected to more open scorn and silent contempt for what was regarded as my hobby and my folly.' Seven years later it was the first building to be acquired by the National Trust. The hall at the centre is open to the rafters and has a floor of rammed chalk, created by tamping down lumps of chalk to a depth of several inches and sealing the mass by flooding it with gallons of sour milk.

He may look 'naked toward the shires', as Kipling wrote, but the Long Man of Wilmington lacks the most celebrated attribute of Cerne Abbas giant in Dorset. Standing some 230ft high, however, his outline now preserved in concrete blocks, he can proudly lay claim to being one of the largest representations of the human form in the world. How long he has been here is unknown (the earliest evidence yet discovered is an early eighteenth century illustration at Chatworth House in Derbyshire) as is the meaning of the 'staves' he holds in his hands, but some scholars plump for the Bronze Age, about four thousand years ago.

The thirteenth century church of St Michael and All Angels, Berwick. After it was damaged by a German bomb during the Second World War, the church was restored under the aegis of Bishop George Bell of Chichester whose memorial in the Cathedral records (among his other attributes) that he was 'a true Pastor, Poet and Patron of the Arts'. The windows, blown out in the blast, were replaced with plain glass, the better to light the wall paintings commissioned from Duncan Grant, Vanessa Bell and her son Quentin Bell.

Left The walled garden at Charleston. Angelica Garnett, Vanessa Bell's daughter by Duncan Grant, was later to write of it: 'Inside it was warm and sheltered, alive with the noises of insects and birds, which sounded different from those outside. In the early morning the sun shone through a milky mist, fragmented into particles of blue and scarlet. As it vanished, the walls began to sing with warmth...'

Below left The Studio at Charleston Farmhouse, on the Gage Estate under Firle Beacon. Vanessa Bell (1879-1961) and Duncan Grant (1885-1978) painted practically every interior surface of the house – walls, doors, beds, cupboards, fire surrounds – and their murals, mosaics, furniture, sculpture and ceramics make Charleston a place of pilgrimage for devotees of the Bloomsbury set.

Right Michelham Priory, seen across the moat from the south, with the east wing of the original thirteenth century priory on the right. Most of the ecclesiastical buildings were reduced to their footings after the Dissolution of the Monasteries, but parts of the remaining walls were later incorporated in the Tudor house we see today. The impressive stone gateway and the monks' stewpond have survived from the early period, while the great barn of oak and elm dates from the sixteenth century. Thomas Child, who came here in 1791, started a large breeding industry for the red Sussex Cattle (now a rare breed), and some of his farm buildings are used as the Michelham tea room and restaurant.

The Bluebell Walk, Arlington. Bluebells thrive in the dappled light of coppice woodland, and every May for years past John McCutchan of Bates Green Farm has opened his 25-acre chestnut wood to the public. An award-winning conservationist, Mr McCutchan erects small boards describing the various habitats within the wood, and the plants and animals which have colonised them.

THE CONQUEST COAST

THE CONQUEST COAST

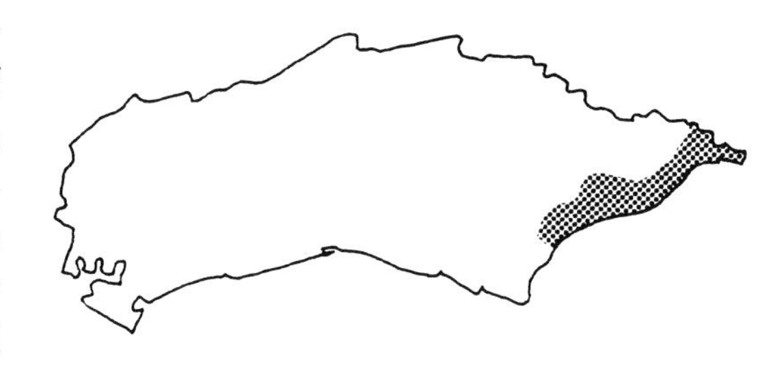

It was at Senlac Hill, six miles north west of Hastings, that William of Normandy defeated the English under Harold on October 14, 1066, and today's promoters of the area are understandably eager to capitalise on the most famous date in English history. They undoubtedly have good reason: the battlefield can be walked in the extensive grounds of Battle Abbey, with explanatory boards showing the positions of the two armies at different stages of the day-long conflict, and a plaque in the ruined abbey church records the very spot where Harold fell. High on the cliffs above Hastings stand the remnants of the great castle the Normans later built to subdue the local populace, carving a huge ditch through the sandstone rock in order to create an impregnable island site for it.

Yet the '1066 Country' slogan does less than justice to the breadth of history and the variety of attractions to be discovered along the county's easternmost shoreline. Hastings itself, for instance, has a colourful fishing quarter and a cramped Old Town between two hills, with steps climbing from its ancient thoroughfares to sequestered courtyards and gardens which make use of every available space. St Leonards, although it now merges almost imperceptibly with its elderly neighbour, still shows signs of its origins as the first purpose-built seaside resort: the London builder James Burton, responsible for a great

Previous page Hastings may mean history for many of its visitors, but it also has a brasher amusements area at the eastern end of its seafront.

De La Warr Pavilion, Bexhill. In a town known for its gentility, it is hardly surprising that the locals generally have a less than respectful attitude towards this striking 1930s building, designed by Erich Mendelsohn and Serge Chermayeff and quite unlike anything else along the seafront. It is, nevertheless, highly regarded in architectural circles: Nairn and Pevsner thought it 'as exhilarating today as when it was new and a revolution for the English seaside.'

A quiet day in Bexhill. The Old Town developed inland, around the parish church of St Peter and the manor house (whose remains can still be seen), and it was as recently as the 1880s that the De La Warr family began to develop the place as a seaside resort. Its heyday was the Edwardian era, when it staged motor racing trials and sanctioned mixed bathing.

many prestigious villas and terraces in the capital, began developing a narrow wooded valley to the west of Hastings in 1828 after having a vivid dream of a 'Regent's Park by the Sea'. The first house erected at St Leonards was his own (made in his London workshop and transported in sections by sea) and it still stands on the seafront as No. 57 Marina.

The towns to either side of the Hastings conurbation could hardly be more different. Bexhill, to the west, was a jaunty place in its Victorian and Edwardian heyday, when it was the first resort to sanction mixed bathing and to organise motor racing trials, but it now offers visitors an air of slumbering gentility. To the east we come first to Winchelsea, a remarkable thirteenth century griddle-pattern town left behind by the retreating sea, and then to incomparable Rye which, with its cobbled streets and ancient fortifications, stands high above the marshes on a sandstone hill.

The beaches of East Sussex are predominantly covered by extensive deposits of shingle, but the wide expanse of sand at Camber provides a notable exception to the rule. This rare blessing may have spawned the less than lovely rash of chalets, bungalows and holiday camps in the area, but ecologists prize the sand dunes immediately seaward of the coast road as among the finest in Sussex.

RX 52
RX53
RX37
RX59
RX76
FE190

Left Fishermen's Beach, Hastings. Devastating storms during the thirteenth century completed the silting up of the harbour at Hastings, but the town has maintained its fishing fleet against all the odds. The fishermen pull their boats up along the eastern foreshore in an area known as The Stade. Their tall, black 'net shops', wooden buildings for storing their nets and other equipment, have stood here (albeit rebuilt after fires and other disasters) for centuries. Close by, maintaining the salty theme, are a Fishermen's Museum, Shipwreck Heritage Centre and Sea Life Centre. The 'RX' painted on the boats signifies that they are registered along the coast at Rye.

Right East Hill Lift, Hastings. One of the steepest of its kind in England, with a gradient of 1/1.28, it opened to the public in 1903 and saves a climb of 272 steps up the honeycombed sandstone cliff to the glorious five-mile stretch of Hastings Country Park. Until it was electrified in 1974, this was one of the last water-balance cliff railways in the country, with water tanks holding 600 gallons.

Below High Street, Hastings. Two ancient thoroughfares (High Street and All Saints Street) run either side of the main road which turns north from the seafront towards Rye. Although Hastings was heavily bombed during the last war, many timber-framed buildings survive. The raised pavement is itself a listed architectural feature.

Left The site of the famous 1066 battlefield, with Battle Abbey behind. Harold's army held the high ground just in front of the Abbey, which was built by William in thanksgiving for his victory. A plaque in the ruined church marks the spot where Harold fell. Today, mock battles are frequently staged here, and our picture shows a commemoration of battles through the ages.

Above The remains of the monks' dormitory at Battle Abbey. Although this thirteenth century building is little more than a roofless shell, it has an atmospheric vaulted undercroft. The Abbey church and most of the other religious buildings were destroyed at the Dissolution of the Monasteries when Henry VIII's Master of the Horse, Sir Anthony Browne, took possession. The great gatehouse survived, however, and Sir Anthony adapted the abbot's house for his mansion. In 1857 this was transformed into the neo-Gothic building which is now Battle Abbey School.

Left Strand Gate, Winchelsea. This remarkable little place is a thirteenth century town planner's dream preserved almost intact because of natural and man-made disasters. The rare grid pattern of its streets was devised in the reign of Edward I when the important port of Old Winchelsea, close to the water's edge, was on the point of destruction by a rapidly encroaching sea. By this time it had become a member of the powerful Cinque Ports Confederation, providing the King with ships for his navy in return for considerable privileges. New Winchelsea was meant to replace the original port, but first the French attacked it, destroying many of its new buildings, and then the sea withdrew, silting up the River Brede and leaving the port marooned inland. The town, never completed, gradually decayed, although three of its ancient gateways still survive. Today it's a delightful spot, with well maintained houses standing on twelve of the thirty-nine squares originally intended by Edward's planners.

Below left Court Hall, Winchelsea. Although it was drastically restored during the sixteenth century, this is one of the oldest buildings in Winchelsea and may even incorporate parts of a farm which existed here before the town was built at the end of the thirteenth century. Winchelsea, despite its small size, still proudly elects a Mayor and Corporation, and the Court Hall is their meeting place. The lower rooms, once the town gaol, are not open to the public, but the upper floor houses a museum of local history.

Upper right Sheep on the levels behind Winchelsea Beach. Hundreds of years ago this area was covered by the sea. East of Winchelsea the flatlands spread across the Kent border to Romney Marsh, which has given its name to a hardy breed of sheep.

Right The medieval town of Rye rises above the marshes on a lofty sandstone ridge with the parish church at its summit. The twelfth century Ypres Tower (now a museum), the sturdy fourteenth century Landgate and remnants of the old town walls are a reminder of times when raids by the French were commonplace. Within the confines of those walls, narrow streets climb the hill, many of them cobbled. Rye became a member of the Cinque Ports Confederation during the twelfth century, and there are echoes of its proud shipbuilding days among the ancient workshops and warehouses of Strand Quay. With the silting of the harbour during the latter part of the sixteenth century the town's seafaring reputation declined, but its later architecture shows that it remained a prosperous country town.

Mermaid Street, Rye. This cobbled street lined with ancient houses has appeared in many films demanding period colour. The Mermaid Inn, near the top of the street on the left-hand side, was once the haunt of the fearsome Hawkhurst Gang – smugglers renowned for the cruelty with which they treated their enemies.

Lamb House, Rye, built in 1723 for the thirteen times mayor of Rye, James Lamb. Two twentieth century writers are associated with the house: E.F.Benson (1867-1940), who set his Mapp and Lucia novels in the town (which he called Tilling) and, immediately before him, the great American-born writer Henry James (1843-1916). Now owned by the National Trust, it contains various James memorabilia, although the Garden Room in which he wrote was destroyed by a bomb during the Second World War.

THE LOW WEALD

THE LOW WEALD

BEFORE the age of the turnpikes Sussex was notorious for the impassability of its roads. Daniel Defoe, travelling through the county in the 1720s, reported seeing, near Lewes, 'an ancient lady, and a lady of very good quality, I assure you, drawn to church in her coach with six oxen; nor was it done in frolic or humour, but mere necessity, the way being so stiff and deep, that no horses could go in it.' At nearby Ringmer Sir Herbert Springett went two better by harnessing eight oxen to his cart when he travelled the two miles to church from Broyle Place.

This inhospitable terrain was the Low Weald, a belt of heavy clay with occasional seams of sandy loam which, running west from the Pevensey Levels, lies immediately beneath the steep scarp face of the South Downs. The soil grows immense oaks, but it presents wretched difficulties for the farmer. The writer Ben Darby has vividly caught its chief characteristics: 'It holds the frost and fog in winter and it parches and cracks quickly in drought, when the heat strikes up into your face from the hot earth.' Rivers and streams which run swiftly from their sources among the high forest ridges, slow to a sluggish pace through this gently undulating land.

Settlements mushroomed around the railway in the central part of this region, and the employment offered by Gatwick Airport to the north has encouraged the further spread of a formless, almost unbroken, urban sprawl from Haywards Heath south through

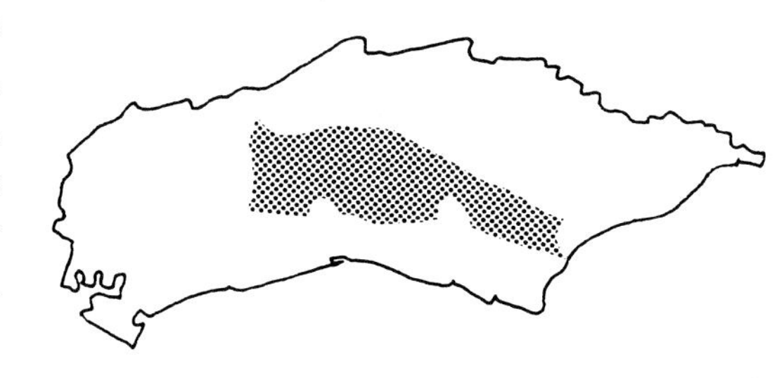

Previous page Shipley windmill. Hilaire Belloc (1870-1953) owned this striking smock mill (so called because its shape is reminiscent of the traditional countryman's working garment), and he lived in the large house nearby. There's a plaque to him inside the mill, and a small exhibition illustrating his life. Built in 1879, this is the youngest of Sussex smock mills, and in its heyday it had the advantage over its rivals of housing a steam engine to drive the machinery when there was no wind. It stopped grinding commercially in 1926, but is open some Sundays during the season.

Above The 'dim blue goodness of the Weald', looking north from Ditchling Beacon.

Left Pevensey Levels. These marshes, once regularly washed by the sea, have for centuries been drained by a network of dykes. With modern, highly efficient pump drainage threatening to dry out the land to the detriment of its rich and diverse wildlife, conservation bodies have acquired parts of the Levels and are farming them in the traditional way.

Burgess Hill to Hassocks. Towns can, of course, be delightful places to visit, but in this region it is the villages which lure the traveller. Even within the shadow of Haywards Heath, the cuckoo which has crowded them to the very edge of their nest, Lindfield and Cuckfield retain their identities, with clusters of fine old buildings to show that they were established long before the navvies got to work with pick and spade. Elsewhere there are many small and attractive villages to be found, 'lost' along winding lanes which have often sunk several feet below the level of the surrounding fields owing to the centuries-long tramp of man and beast over the sticky, yielding clay.

Pevensey Castle. The Romans built a fort at Pevensey as the last and largest of their Saxon Shore defences between Norfolk and the Isle of Wight, but after the legions left Britain it was overrun by land-hungry invaders. According to the *Anglo Saxon Chronicle*, an army under Aelle besieged the fort in 491 'and slew all the inhabitants; there was not even one Briton left there.' Centuries later the conquering Normans repaired the defences, built a castle inside them and founded a small town on the outside. Although there are substantial remains from both periods today, the sea which once lapped the walls has gone – retreating by about a mile to leave this once mighty fortress high and dry.

The church of St Mary the Virgin at Westham, adjoining Pevensey, is claimed to be the first built by the Normans after their invasion of 1066. Four unmarked stones in the churchyard indicate the communal burial ground of people who died of the Plague in 1666.

Herstmonceux Castle, built of Flemish bricks in 1440, was more of a manor house than a fortification, despite its moat, 4ft-thick walls and gatehouse with gun and arrow loops. It was built for Sir Roger de Fiennes, who served with Henry V at Agincourt. Today it's owned by Queen's University, Ontario, which opens the grounds to the public during the season.

This series of empty green domes in the grounds of Herstmonceux Castle is a rather eerie reminder that the Royal Greenwich Observatory came here in 1948 to escape the bright lights and polluted skies of London. In 1967 the Queen opened the Isaac Newton telescope here, but by the 1980s the astronomers were making far greater use of their telescope on the island of La Palma in the Canaries, and at the end of the decade the decision was taken to move the observatory to Cambridge.

Trug-making at the Sussex Trugs Ltd factory, Herstmonceux. The split-wood baskets now indispensable for gardeners were invented in the village by Thomas Smith in 1829, and the last of the Smith line, 86-year-old Raymond, is still working for the firm part-time and training young craftsmen. The Sussex Trugs factory produces some 14,000 baskets a year using willow for the boards and chestnut for the handle and rim.

The pond at Lindfield, one of the loveliest of Sussex villages.

Ouse Valley Viaduct, Balcombe. John Raistrick's 1475ft creation, with its 37 arches and its stone pavilions, is one of the glories of the railway age in Sussex. The London-to-Brighton railway line was completed in 1841.

Christ's Hospital School, near Itchingfield. The school, founded in London by Edward VI in 1553, moved out to Sussex as recently as 1902. This green field site was to spawn a veritable small town, with a large central quad entered via two gateways. In 1951 pupils from the Bluecoat School in Chichester, founded by Oliver Whitby in 1702, transferred to Christ's Hospital – bringing with them its now commonly used alternative name. The school, which is a charitable organisation giving independent education to youngsters unlikely to be offered it elsewhere, takes more than 800 boarders of both sexes. Christ's Hospital has strong musical and artistic traditions, and each day the school band plays pupils into lunch in the dining hall.

Left Taking a fence at the All England Show Jumping Course, Hickstead.

Below Brewers Yard, Storrington – a village which, like many in Sussex, has almost grown into a town, but not quite.

Below A view along Cuckfield High Street. Local landowners refused to countenance a railway station in the 1840s, and the growth of nearby Haywards Heath as a commuter town was the result. Like Lindfield to the east, Cuckfield feels the press of the sprawling upstart community on its doorstep but has managed to retain something of its character and individuality.

The Blue Idol meeting house at Coneyhurst, originally a farmhouse but acquired by the Society of Friends in 1691 at a time when Quakers were being persecuted for their beliefs. The Quaker founder of Pennsylvania, William Penn (1644-1718) used to walk the few miles from his home at Warminghurst in order to join in the services here. The name defeats everyone, the best bet being that it refers to the period from 1793 until 1869 when the building lay idle and was colour-washed in blue.

The 'Prayer Book' interior of the thirteenth century church of the Holy Sepulchre, Warminghurst, with its box pews, three-decker pulpit and Queen Anne coat-of-arms on the tympanum of the chancel screen. The Victorians, keen to emphasise ritual rather than preaching, stripped most of our churches of what they saw as irrelevant furniture, and few remain in this unspoiled eighteenth century state. William Penn lived in a house across the fields from here, and a few fragments of its walls can still be seen.

Parham House, under the Downs near Storrington. Built by the London merchant Sir Thomas Palmer in 1577, it is approached through a vast and ancient deer park. Inside the house there is a collection of Elizabethan and Stuart portraits, china, tapestries, oriental carpets and furniture, but the most magical effect is produced by the Long Gallery with its views across the park to the Downs. Stretching for all of 160ft, this was sufficiently ample to accommodate the Parham Troop of Yeomanry at their drill practice during the Napoleonic wars.

The church of St Peter, Parham, the sole remnant of an inconvenient little village removed from the grounds of the house during the eighteenth century. It retains its box pews and a squire's pew complete with fireplace.

THE WESTERN WEALD
MIDHURST AND PETWORTH

THE WESTERN WEALD
MIDHURST AND PETWORTH

THE north-west corner of Sussex, an unkempt land of heather, bracken and pine, is quite unlike any other part of the county. 'I have never,' wrote William Cobbett, who had an aversion to untamed countryside, 'seen the earth flung about in such a wild way.' The poet Tennyson, one of the many who have loved this sandy heathland with its distant views of the sea, built a house on Black Down which, at 919ft, is the highest point in Sussex: he and his wife Emily used to go to church at Lurgashall, one of several beautiful villages which lie under the hill, and the lectern commemorates them.

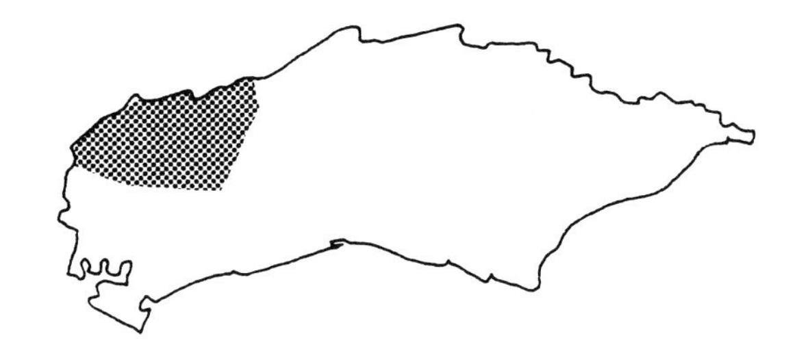

The soil in this Surrey border country is lower greensand, and below the great massif of Black Down stretches a broad scattering of heathy commons and pinewoods which extends south towards the Rother Valley and re-establishes itself below Midhurst and Petworth. No longer controlled by traditional cutting and grazing, the landscape is swiftly colonised by scrub and seedling trees, but the areas of dry acid heath which are protected as nature reserves (among them the commons at Iping, Stedham, Ambersham, Lavington, Coates and Wiggonholt) are ideal territory for snakes and lizards and a teeming community of insects and spiders.

Previous page A sunken track on Black Down, the highest point in Sussex. The poet, Lord Tennyson, built a house here with a distant view of the sea.

West Sussex was always more feudal than East, a fact symbolised by the way the old buildings of Petworth press, as if for protection, close to the walls of the ancient seat of the Percy family. With its twisting streets leading to a handsome market square, this small and compact town should certainly be explored for its own sake, but it is Petworth House, its grounds transformed by Capability Brown, which dominates the place as it has done for centuries. Its front has been likened to a chateau in the grand manner of Louis XIV's France, and its treasures include woodcarvings by Grinling Gibbons and paintings by Van Dyck, William Blake and Turner, who produced a large number of landscapes while working here. Constable, who also found a patron at Petworth, thought the place uncomfortably cold.

Heyshott Common, with a prospect of the Downs to the south. The dry sandy commons in the north-west of Sussex are rich in insect life.

Midhurst, a few miles to the west, has its feudal touches, too. Yellow paintwork on cottages and other buildings in the area testifies to ownership by the Cowdray Estate, whose reach extends to Cowdray Park, where polo is played in the summer, and to the picturesque ruins of the great Elizabethan mansion of Cowdray. Midhurst is a spacious and comfortable town, with a host of timber-framed buildings. It hides the best grouping in the maze-like thoroughfares between South Street and Knockhundred Row, where you'll find some lovely tile-hung cottages, the sixteenth century market hall and the Spread Eagle Inn, parts of which date from the early sixteenth century. The Grammar School in North Street, founded in 1672, counts among its famous pupils the novelist H. G. Wells, who worked as an apprentice in a chemist's shop nearby.

Above Cowdray Ruins. Sir Anthony Browne, who had been granted Battle Abbey at the Dissolution of the Monasteries, acquired the splendid Cowdray House in 1542 and put the finishing touches to a building which had been begun at the end of the previous century. A monk is said to have put a curse on Sir Anthony for his treatment of the Abbey church to the effect that his line would perish through fire and water. This obviously took some time to work, but within the space of eight days in 1793 the house burned down and the last of the family drowned while trying to shoot falls on the Rhine. The ruins are approached across a causeway from the car park at the Easebourne end of Midhurst.

Right The Western Rother at Lower Fittleworth, a short distance before it joins the Arun.

The uncompromisingly noble west front of Petworth House. Although traces of an original twelfth century house can still be made out, this is the work of the sixth Duke of Somerset between 1688 and 1696. The Wyndham family, to whom the estate passed in 1750, made further significant changes: the second Earl of Egremont employed the young Capability Brown to landscape the Park, while the third Earl (legendary for both his patronage of the arts and his agricultural improvements) made significant additions to the house's collections of furniture, paintings and sculpture. Petworth's treasures include works by Turner, Blake, Van Dyck and Hieronymus Bosch and intricate carvings in lime wood by the great Grinling Gibbons. The 700-acre Park, open to the public free of charge, is home to a herd of two hundred fallow deer.

East Street, Petworth. The ornate lamp standard at the junction with North Street, was designed by Sir Charles Barry, architect of the new Houses of Parliament. He had been brought in to restore the church and is responsible for the warm red brick of the upper tower. It was originally stuccoed and sported a spire, but the spire proved too frail and the stucco was stripped away.

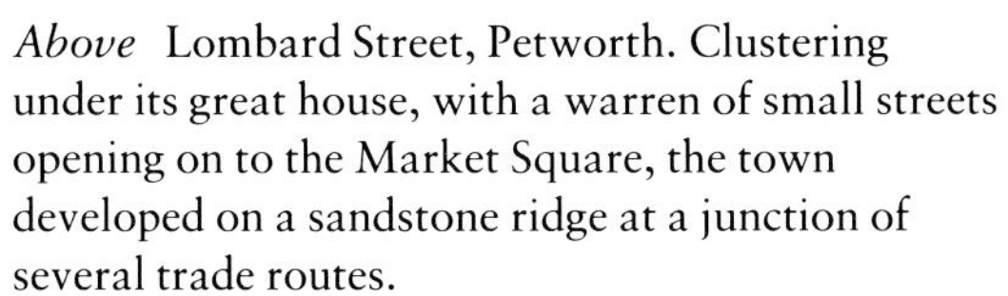
Above Lombard Street, Petworth. Clustering under its great house, with a warren of small streets opening on to the Market Square, the town developed on a sandstone ridge at a junction of several trade routes.

Below Burton Pond. Originally created to power the machines of the Wealden iron industry (cast-iron Tudor cannon were manufactured here), later used to turn the wheel of an eighteenth century water mill, Burton Pond is now a nature reserve. A circular trail of 2 miles passes by open water, reedbed, bog and woodland, and the County Council's trail guide points out a prodigious variety of wildlife.

Above The Swan at Lower Fittleworth, which the writer E.V. Lucas thought 'the most ingeniously placed inn in the world,' with a water mill and an ancient bridge close by. The visitors' books reveal that the Swan has long been a popular haunt for writers and artists.

Knockhundred Row, Midhurst. There's much more to Midhurst than a motorist would guess from simply driving along its broad main street. Knockhundred Row leads to Market Square and an attractive grouping of fine old buildings, some of them medieval.

Polo at Cowdray Park.

ASHDOWN FOREST AND THE HIGH WEALD

ASHDOWN FOREST AND THE HIGH WEALD

FROM the honeycombed cliffs of Hastings a broad belt of hard and ancient sandstone irregularly seamed with far softer clay swings north and west to Ashdown Forest and beyond. This is the High Weald, an area of dramatic beauty whose geological substrata have created a landscape of steep hills and lofty ridges intercut by deep valleys. Many of the finest villages of this region sit high above a countryside of woods and small farms, the lanes that connect them following a narrow and winding course between high and grassy banks. Rotherfield and Mayfield are both hilltop settlements, while Ticehurst and Wadhurst run along an east-west ridge close to the Kent border and Burwash hugs the crest of another further to the south. The market town of Heathfield climbs towards this ridge, with its half-forgotten precursor, Old Heathfield, a mile or so away on the far side of Heathfield Park.

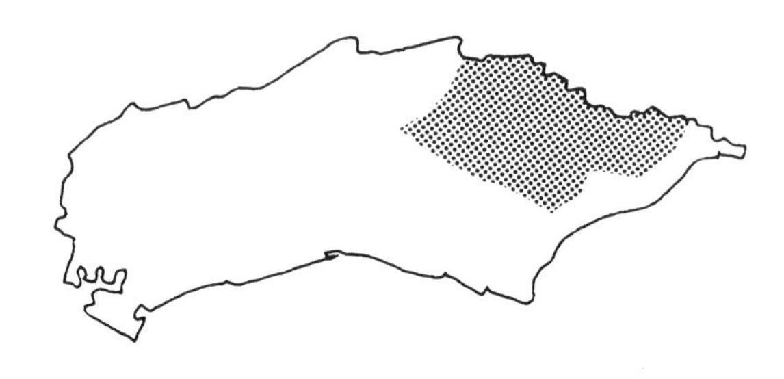

In moist High Weald ravines where streams splash over the rocks beneath an overhang of trees, botanists have identified an unlikely collection of ferns, mosses and other plants which are otherwise found only on the sea-washed west coast of England and Scotland:

Previous page Ashdown Forest, near Wych Cross. The forest comprises five per cent of the entire lowland heath of Britain.

Above Pooh Bridge, near Hartfield. Winnie the Pooh, Christopher Robin and their friends had their adventures at 'an enchanted place' on Ashdown Forest, and this is the spot at which they played the simple, and irresistible, game of 'Pooh-sticks'. The not-so-young-at-heart may need reminding that competitors lean over the bridge to drop a twig upriver, then rush to the other side to see which emerges first on the current. At Gills Lap ('Galleons Lap' in the books) there is a memorial plaque to A. A. Milne and his illustrator, E. H. Shepard.

Left The brilliance of flowering gorse by a ride on Ashdown Forest. Although there are several wooded areas on the forest, the Conservators charged with caring for it keep large tracts free of encroaching bracken, birch and Scots pine in order to encourage heathland plants and their associated wildlife. At one time the vegetation was kept low by commoners, who had rights to collect small wood and graze their animals on the heath.

these are almost certainly the relics of an original flora which died out in the rest of lowland Britain thousands of years ago, but which has heroically managed to survive in these conveniently damp surroundings. The streams, dammed to form pond-bays, were once vital to the iron-making industry which had its centre here, and names on the map will lead you to the sites: Furnace Lane, Hammerpond, Minepit Wood. At Wadhurst the church has more than thirty cast-iron memorial slabs set into its floor, their dates ranging from 1617 to 1799.

The ironmasters managed considerable areas of regenerating coppice woodland to produce the charcoal for their furnaces, but large parts of Ashdown Forest have been bare of trees for many centuries. It was the obstinate commoners, resisting moves to enclose their land, who ensured that we have this lovely exposed heathland to enjoy today. In 1693, after a bitter struggle in which they tore down fences and uprooted newly-planted hedges, a Royal Commission upheld their rights to cut bracken and litter for bedding their animals; to use birch trees for firewood, fence repairs and the construction of their hovels; and to graze their cattle over an area of 6,400 acres. This activity created the tousled heathland of ling, gorse and purple moor grass which conservationists preserve today through a never-ending programme of cutting back the scrub and bracken and weeding out the invasive silver birch and Scots pine. The Forest, constituting five per cent of Britain's remaining lowland heath, is designated as a Site of Special Scientific Interest within an Area of Outstanding Natural Beauty.

Above Bayham Abbey. The prettiest monastic ruins in the county lie beside the Teise stream, a tributary of the Medway which is here the boundary between Sussex and Kent. The Premonstratensian abbey dates from the thirteenth century, and a considerable amount of the church and its surrounding buildings still remains. A picturesque separate gatehouse to the north-west stands on the very edge of the stream and, although the water close by is often lined with fishermen, patient gazing through one of the windows may be rewarded with the sight of a kingfisher. When the Abbey was closed down by Cardinal Wolsey in 1525 the canons and their servants were involved in an armed sit-in, their protest leading to imprisonment for the ringleaders.

Above Nutley post mill is almost certainly the oldest of its kind in Sussex, a county peculiarly rich in windmills. Of the three main types of mill (the others are tower and smock), the post is the most primitive: the whole building swings around a huge central pillar so that the sweeps, as the sails are known in Sussex, face the wind. Probably built at the end of the seventeenth century, Nutley Mill was completely restored in 1973 by the Uckfield and District Preservation Society, work which earned an Architectural Heritage Year Award two years later.

Right Bewl Water. This huge reservoir, covering 770 acres and with a capacity of 6,900 million gallons, is the largest expanse of water in south-east England. It was built between 1973 and 1975 in order to provide water for the Medway towns: the main entrance was then in Kent, but a change in boundaries has since brought the whole of the reservoir into Sussex. Some areas are given over to fishing, sailing, rowing and scuba diving, and a nature reserve occupies more than a hundred acres of the reservoir's central arm.

Bodiam Castle. It may be little more than a shell today, but this is undoubtedly everyone's idea of a fairy-tale castle. It was built by Sir Edward Dalyngrigge at the end of the fourteenth century, when attacks by French pirates sailing up the then easily navigable River Rother were an everyday danger. A hollow in the bank of the moat south of the Castle is thought to have been a harbour deep enough for two warships. The main gate was heavily defended. A bridge now crosses the moat in a straight line, but excavations have revealed that attackers would once have needed to negotiate a series of them, first crossing from the west to the octagonal stone islet in the centre and so exposing themselves to fire on their right-hand side. If they did manage to reach the gateway (always under fire from bombards, an early form of cannon) they would have to pass under an arched opening through which the defenders would rain missiles upon their heads. After that they would meet a series of portcullises, again suffering assault from above through circular openings in the ceiling called 'meurtrieres' or murder holes. As it happens, however, the Castle was never attacked.

Left Pastureland at Wallcrouch, between Wadhurst and Ticehurst. Oast houses like those on the left of the picture are a common feature of the Kent border country, although the growing of hops for the brewing industry has now almost disappeared.

Above Bateman's at Burwash (built for a seventeenth century ironmaster) was Rudyard Kipling's home from 1902 until his death thirty-four years later, and the interior remains very much as he knew it. The study, for instance, seems eternally to await his return, with all his books on the shelves, the Indian rugs especially woven for him, his huge wastepaper basket and the desk littered with his accumulated writer's paraphernalia of paperweight, pen tray, ruler and the like. The grounds reveal the Kipling touch, too. He and his wife Carrie designed the rose garden and created the pond, while the watermill (though now restored and grinding corn) still has the turbine which the writer installed to drive a generator that produced electric lighting for the house. Kipling was a keen early motorist, and one of his gleaming Rolls Royces can be seen in the garage.

Left Typical Wealden houses, tile-hung and weather-boarded, in the High Street at Burwash.

Above The High Street at Mayfield, now happily bypassed. The Victorian writer Coventry Patmore thought it 'the sweetest village in England'.

Upper right St Dunstan and the Devil confront one another underneath the name on the Mayfield village sign. The saint, a blacksmith by trade, was born in the village, built its first wooden church in 960 AD and – after becoming Archbishop of Canterbury – founded the Old Palace, whose remains lie within the convent at the top of the hill. Legend has it that the Devil came to Dunstan's forge in the tempting guise of a pretty girl, but the saint spotted a tell-tale cloven hoof and seized his enemy's nose in a pair of glowing tongs. The Devil was forced to promise that he would never enter a house which had a horseshoe above its door.

Right Colin West fashioning a cricket bat at the Gray-Nicolls factory, Robertsbridge. The business dates from 1876 when a local enthusiast, Levi Nicolls, began making bats for his cricketing friends. Not only did the great Dr W.G.Grace prove their worth by using them in all his important matches (he scored a thousand runs in May with one of them), but world-class batsmen are still ordering them from Robertsbridge today. It was with a tailor-made Gray-Nicolls 'Scoop' bat that Brian Lara smote 375 for the West Indies against England in Antigua in April, 1994, quickly following that feat with a score of 501 not out (a county championship record) for Warwickshire.

Above Cade Street Chapel. Early non-conformism flourished in the east of Sussex, with a great many dissenters to be found among small tradesmen and craftsmen. The chapel at Cade Street, on the borders of Heathfield parish, was built in 1809 to replace an earlier one along the road at Punnett's Town.

Left The thirteenth century church of All Saints, Old Heathfield. The modern market town of Heathfield grew up around the railway, now gone, leaving Old Heathfield in attractive isolation some 1 ½ miles to the east. Several gravestones in the churchyard are decorated with the unique terra-cotta plaques produced by the local mason and potter Jonathan Harmer (1763-1849), who lived close by in Portland Square, and whose designs featured cherubs, vases, baskets of fruit or figures of Faith, Hope and Charity.

Upper right The Sugar Loaf at Wood's Corner. The Brightling area is littered with the follies of the local squire and MP John 'Mad Jack' Fuller (1757-1834). A substantial man in several senses of the word – rich, influential, exceedingly fat – he saved Bodiam Castle from demolition, commissioned the artist Turner to paint local scenes, hired the landscape gardener Humphry Repton, and probably devised some of his odd buildings partly in order to give local men work to do at a time of economic recession. The Sugar Loaf was supposedly run up very quickly after Fuller rashly bet a carousing visitor that he could see the spire of Dallington church from an upstairs window. When the cold light of day proved otherwise, he arranged for this look-alike to be erected before his friend should come again. The folly was once inhabited: a chimney protruded from the stonework, and the postman used to call.

Right Fuller's curious pyramidal mausoleum in Brightling churchyard. Inside the church is the barrel organ he had installed with great ceremony, presenting the male members of the choir with white smocks, buskin breeches and yellow stockings and the girls with red cloaks.

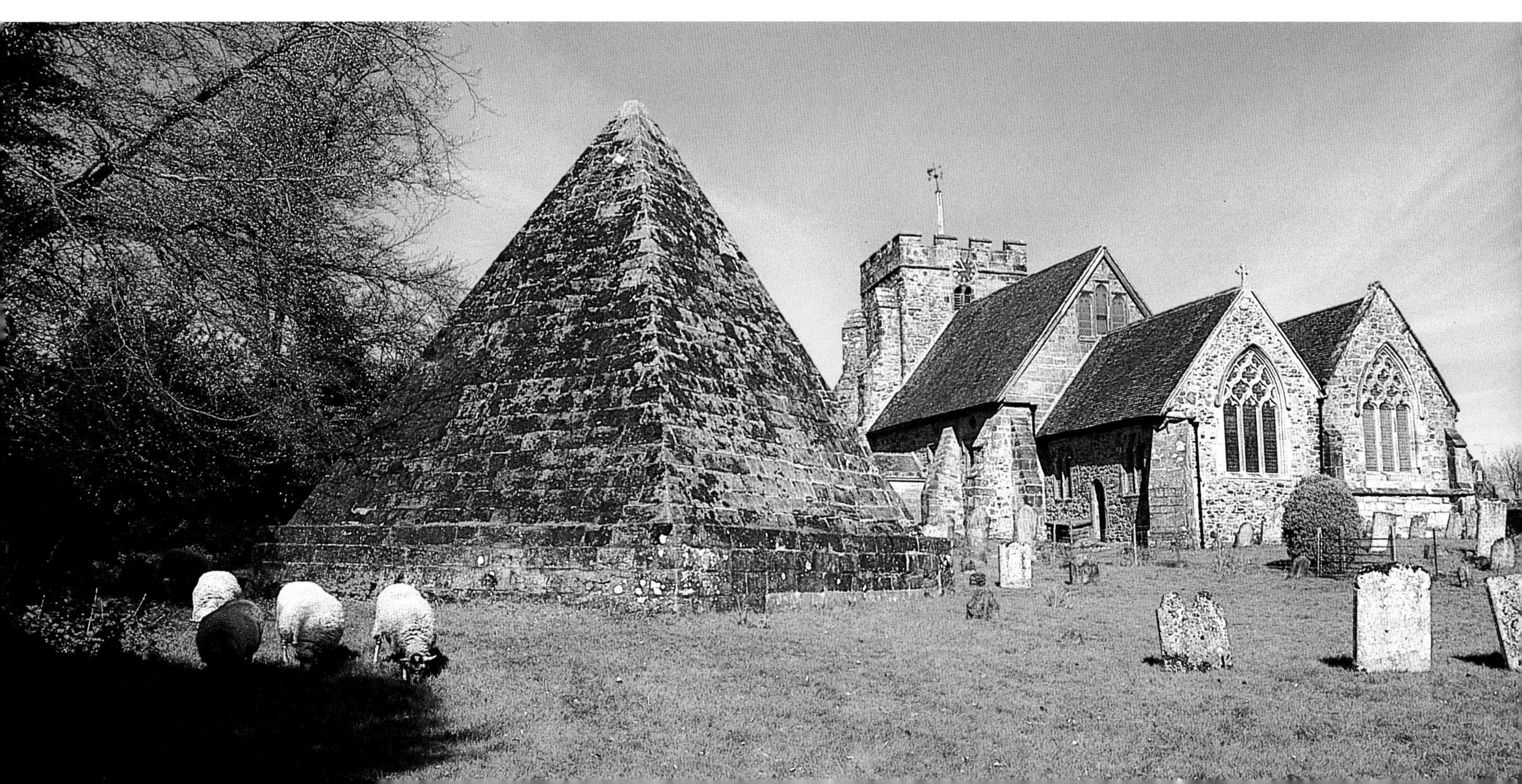

Great Dixter, Northiam. Two houses have become one: the London merchant Nathaniel Lloyd had a medieval hall house from Kent (on the right of the picture) transplanted across the border and attached to the larger one he bought here in 1910. The architect Sir Edwin Lutyens oversaw the operation and also designed the gardens. The Lloyd family still owns the property, which is open to the public during the season, and the grounds are managed by the gardening writer Christopher Lloyd.

Well-house on the village green, Sedlescombe.

THE FOREST RIDGE
EAST GRINSTEAD
HORSHAM AND CRAWLEY

THE FOREST RIDGE, EAST GRINSTEAD, HORSHAM & CRAWLEY

WEST of Ashdown Forest the sandstone country stretches some twelve miles from East Grinstead to Horsham, an area of woods, steep valleys and scattered rock outcrops known as the Forest Ridge – although the countryside is, in fact, corrugated by a number of parallel ridges. This is where the great Wealden gardens are to be found, some of them internationally famous. At Wakehurst Place, Sheffield Park, Leonardslee, Nymans, Borde Hill and High Beeches the acid soil grows profuse rhododendrons and azaleas, camellias and magnolias.

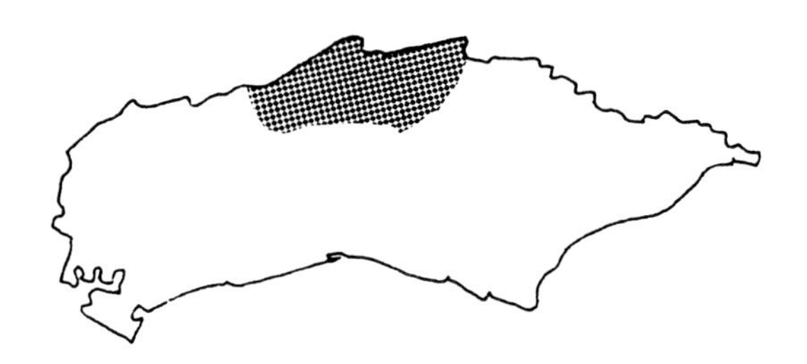

Two ancient settlements stand at either end of this territory, with a much younger but now considerably larger one between. East Grinstead, mentioned in Domesday, a substantial place during the Middle Ages and an assize town until 1799, has a handsome High Street with some of its older buildings (including the church and the seventeenth century Sackville College almshouses) fashioned from local stone. Horsham, the second town of West Sussex after Chichester, not only held assizes but was the site of the county

Previous page Herbaceous borders at Nymans Garden, Handcross. Although it has been owned by the National Trust since 1954, this garden is a tribute to the work of four generations of the Messel family. Ludwig Messel bought the house and grounds in 1890 and introduced a rich variety of plants gathered from all over the world. An existing orchard was transformed into what was to become the centrepiece of Nymans, the Wall Garden, and he also created the Pinetum, the Heather Garden and the Pergola Walk. His son, Lt.Col. Leonard Messel, who inherited it in 1916, subscribed to many of the Far Eastern and South American plant expeditions of the 1920s, introducing their discoveries to Nymans. He also planted the Top Garden, while his wife created the Rose Garden. The house itself, along with a priceless horticultural library, was largely destroyed by fire in 1947 and was for many years a picturesque ruin open to the sky. In 1995, however, the National Trust decided to renovate the building and use it for displays.

Roost Hole Pond in St Leonard's Forest. The Forest Ridge is scattered with hammer ponds like this – formed by damming streams to power the bellows and hammers of the Wealden iron industry.

gaol from the sixteenth century until just after 1844, when it staged the last of many well-attended public executions. The calcareous sandstone in this region was widely used for the heavy roofing tiles known as Horsham slabs, weighing as much as half a hundredweight each: the resultant sagging roofs can be seen on several timber-framed Wealden houses in the historic Carfax and Causeway area of a town otherwise much changed and looped about with new roads in order to accommodate the demands posed by modern traffic.

Crawley, sprawling between its two seniors, offers a few tantalising reminders of its past along the High Street, where a handful of medieval buildings can be found in the vicinity of the George Hotel, but these traces are swamped by the New Town which was designated in 1947 and which – encouraged by the growth of nearby Gatwick Airport – has rapidly swallowed neighbouring settlements such as Three Bridges, Ifield and Worth. There may be little enough of the typical Wealden greenery here, but the 400 acres of Tilgate Park, just south of the town, are a remarkable public amenity, with gardens, three lakes and a rare breeds centre. This was once a family estate, as was Buchan Country Park to the south west of the town, where the local authority has established a nature trail and, in the information centre, a display of the local flora and fauna.

The hamlet of Worth, ensnared by expanding Crawley within a curve of the M23 motorway, has a rare surprise in store for the unsuspecting visitor – one of the finest Saxon churches in the whole of England, and the only one which retains its original plan of cruciform layout with apsidal chancel.

The tower of St Swithun's church, East Grinstead, is made of the local sandstone, its colour varying from yellow to grey.

Sackville College Almshouses, East Grinstead. The Sackvilles, Earls of Dorset, founded this fine Jacobean building with its quadrangle of low stone buildings round a large central courtyard in 1617, and the family's heraldic leopard rears up from a pagoda-like cupola above the north wing. This part of the building (the Dorset Lodgings) was used by the owners as a hunting lodge and a staging post between London and their Sussex estates, but the rest was permanently occupied by 31 of the local poor who were 'there to live, to pray, serve, honour and praise Almighty God.' Today the College is home to eighteen elderly people, but there are guided tours during the season. In the study is a desk at which the controversial warden, John Mason Neale, wrote the words of 'Good King Wenceslas'. Neale, a scholar, historian and ecclesiologist, was suspected of Popish leanings, and when he erected a rood cross in the chapel he was reported to the bishop. He ignored a subsequent 'inhibition' forbidding him to preach in the College, and passions became so inflamed that attempts were made on his life. The offending cross can still be seen.

Standen, near East Grinstead. One of the more modern properties owned by the National Trust, Standen was built for a London solicitor by the architect Philip Webb in the 1890s. Webb was a friend of the poet, artist and social reformer William Morris, whose wallpapers and textiles are perhaps the outstanding feature of the house. The grounds, on a steep slope with views across the Medway valley to Ashdown Forest, comprise a terrace walk, a rhododendron dell, a quarry garden and an orchard.

Marbles Championships, Tinsley Green. Good Friday is the traditional day for playing marbles in Sussex, and at Tinsley Green near the Surrey border the grandly-named British Marbles Board of Control organises an annual British and World Marbles Championship. Players attempt to knock marbles out of a 6ft-diameter ring.

St Nicholas, Worth, one of the largest and best-preserved Saxon churches in England. Built some time between 950 and 1050 on the basilica plan introduced to this country by St. Augustine, it has an apsidal east end, a massive chancel arch and the full range of late Saxon architectural features. In the churchyard is the grave of Robert Whitehead, inventor of the first successful torpedo.

The Priest House, West Hoathly. The Sussex Archaeological Society owns this fine, medieval timber-framed house, with its wattle and daub walls and a roof made of the heavy sandstone slates known as Horsham slabs. The garden has been planted with the kind of old-fashioned flowers (day lilies, golden rod, hollyhocks) once common in cottage gardens throughout the land.

A school of tailfins at Gatwick International Airport. The airport grew from a pre-1939 airfield on the site of the old Gatwick racecourse and is now one of the busiest in the world, handling more than twenty million passengers a year. The newer of its two main buildings, the North Terminal, was opened by the Queen in 1988.

Queen's Square, Crawley. The bandstand which adds a little grace to the New Town's functional centre once stood on the old Gatwick Racecourse, obliterated to make way for the international airport.

The Causeway, Horsham. 'As an anthology of cosy Wealden buildings it would be hard to beat,' enthused Nairn and Pevsner. The Causeway, hidden away from the town's shopping district, is a leafy avenue leading to the parish church.

Above South of England Show, Ardingly. This annual event of early June brings farmers from all the neighbouring counties to pit their prime livestock against all comers.

Left Ardingly Reservoir. The 189-acre reservoir is fed by the Shell and Ardingly Brooks, tributaries of the Ouse. Its main role is to store water at times of surplus and release it when there are shortages so that more water is available at Barcombe Waterworks 14 miles downstream.

Right Sheffield Park Garden. The variety of trees in this beautiful garden may be gauged from the fact that there are almost two hundred kinds of conifer alone. It has no fewer than four lakes, two created by Capability Brown for the first Earl of Sheffield around 1775, the others (and the dramatic cascade between them) dating from the nineteenth century, when the third Earl planted many exotic trees among Brown's native species. Like all the great Wealden gardens, Sheffield Park has two particularly enchanting periods each year: spring, when the rhododendrons and azaleas are in bloom, and autumn, when the glowing reds, yellows and oranges of the dying leaves are reflected in the waters of the lakes. The neo-Gothic castellations of the privately-owned house where Edward Gibbon wrote parts of *The Decline and Fall of the Roman Empire* are repeatedly glimpsed through the trees.

Above A Q1 class Bullied Pacific on the Bluebell Railway passes under Three Arch Bridge near Horsted Keynes. Since the original Lewes to East Grinstead line was used mainly for freight, it's safe to say that more passengers now use the seven and a half mile section from Horsted Keynes to Newcombe Bridge than at any time in the past. The line was closed in the 1950s, but preservationists soon made it the first restored standard gauge passenger railway to operate with vintage engines and coaches. More land is being steadily acquired, and there are plans eventually to link up with the commercial network at East Grinstead. Meantime, the Bluebell Railway has a small museum and the largest collection of engines in the south dating from 1865 to 1958. This Bullied Pacific, the only surviving example on a preserved railway, once shunted the famous Golden Arrow.

Wakehurst Place, or 'Kew in the Country'. The National Trust owns this property, but the remarkable grounds with their valley, streams, lake and dramatic rock outcrops are leased to the Royal Botanic Gardens. Although the distance from Kew is not very great, the difference in soils and climate is surprisingly marked, allowing a range of plants to be grown here which would never survive in Surrey.

ACKNOWLEDGEMENTS

A large number of people have helped in the creation of this book, and our thanks are due to them all. First and foremost, there are the people of Sussex who by chance appear in the photographs, either wittingly or unwittingly. Then there are those, listed below, who have generously helped by providing facilities for photography not normally available. Our principal regret is that lack of space has meant that we have only been able to include a fraction of the photographs.

A particular debt is owed to booksellers throughout Sussex who have encouraged the project: without their support it would never have been started. More specifically our thanks must also go to the following for their generous help and assistance: Chris & Anne Yarrow of Wilderness Wood; Thomas Smith, trugmakers of Herstmonceux; Harvey's Brewery of Lewes; Miss Emery, the administrator of Uppark House; Colin West of Gray-Nicholls, Robertsbridge; David Atkins and Mrs Jill Belton of Tullens Toat, Pulborough; and Kitty Shepherd (potter), Arthur Haffenden (besoms) and the Chalk Pit Forge all of whom are based at the Amberley Chalk Pits Museum.

We are also grateful to The Charleston Trust for the photograph of the interior of Charleston Farmhouse on page 78, and Joanna Townsend of Glyndebourne Festival Opera for providing the lower two photographs on page 52 (copyright; Guy Gravett from Picture Index).

All the other photographs were taken by Terry Heathcote on Kodachrome 64 film using a Nikon F4S camera and three lenses, ranging from 24mm to 200mm and, during the later stages, a 28mm perspective control lens. Having a preference for natural light and colour, filters were avoided, whilst flash was employed for the few photographs involving craftsmen working indoors. A tripod was essential for all other interior shots where reliance was placed on natural light and for a limited number of exteriors when the situation demanded.

TERRY HEATHCOTE AND DAVID ARSCOTT

INDEX

Hang gliding at Harting Down.